Tom Fahey is a husband, father, and a proud grandfather first and foremost. He is the ultimate sports nut, but not to watch, to participate. After a successful sales management career which took him all over the world, keeping him on planes and in hotels, he has averaged reading 90 books a year for over 40 years, and now, in retirement, is finally working on a promise to write.

To my family, the only reason we are really here.

Tom Fahey

43 DAYS OF REFLECTIONS AND RUMINATIONS

AUSTIN MACAULEY PUBLISHERS™

LONDON • CAMBRIDGE • NEW YORK • SHARJAH

Ordering Information
Quantity sales: Special discounts are available on quantity purchases by corporations, associations, and others. For details, contact the publisher at the address below.

Publisher's Cataloging-in-Publication data
Fahey, Tom
43 Days of Reflections and Ruminations

ISBN 9781638290643 (Paperback)
ISBN 9781638290650 (ePub e-book)

Library of Congress Control Number: 2021925618

www.austinmacauley.com/us

First Published 2022
Austin Macauley Publishers LLC
40 Wall Street, 33rd Floor, Suite 3302
New York, NY 10005
USA

mail-usa@austinmacauley.com
+1 (646) 5125767

Table of Contents

Chapter 1
Childhood

When you start with your childhood story, you really cannot start at childbirth. You may have let out a good scream when slapped on the ass, but no way you can remember that. At best, you will remember stories told of your early years. I have two favorites; early stories that my mom repeated many times. When I was born, she told my spinster Great-Aunt Annie, while still in the hospital, that she really did not want a boy and she could have me. Aunt Annie took that to heart, and I was always her special little boy. The other was that my mom had wrapped me in a blanket, and I was sleeping on the couch when my Uncle Bob came in and was about to plop himself right down on top of me. Mom screamed, and somehow, Uncle Bob stopped in midair avoiding a quick end to my very short existence. Of course, I only remember these stories because I heard them at every family gathering for twenty years.

I define my childhood as all the first twelve plus years we spent in my hometown of Rushville, Indiana. Rushville was founded in the 1820s, and with the arrival of the railroad in 1850, it quickly grew to a dynamic small town with banks, factories, mills, and grain elevators. The Rush County had excellent crop ground and a mix of hardwood forests for furniture manufacturing, both of which were critical for its early development. With three large furniture manufacturing plants and a foundry, it had jobs for young men like my father looking for good employment after WWII. The Durbin Hotel in Rushville was the campaign headquarters for Wendell Willkie's failed presidential campaign against Franklin D. Roosevelt.

I was born in 1953, which was pretty much the economic peak in Rushville's history. Shortly after that, they witnessed the slow steady decline that was occurring in many small rural American towns. I think two keys especially contributed to the decline of Rushville. First, the interstate system missed us, and manufacturing started its slow and steady move overseas. Our census was over seven thousand in 1960, but the following three decades were all steady declines. I did not know it then, but I grew up in one of the best possible times for small-town America.

When I try to focus on my childhood, there are general impressions like I had loving parents and great relatives as well as a fun and well-rounded life. I think that type of childhood is more the norm in America than the TV or press understands. But when I really try to dig into my memories, it is like looking at a steamed-over mirror after a very hot shower. The mirror is fogged, and if I take the tip of my finger and touch it dozens of times, there are tiny clear areas. These small spots are like specific memories. But really, most of my childhood is a condensation of recollections such as playing baseball, going to the county fair, or weekends out at my great-aunt's farms. I want to share some of the general recollections as well as clear snapshots that are burned into my early memories.

We lived on 1116 N. Arthur Street; funny how I just remembered that address without even thinking. Our back fence was adjacent to the county fairgrounds and less than two blocks to a city park. What a fertile playground for a boy with a bike and a BB gun. To this day, I believe I snuck into the fairground's old buildings more than any other Rushville resident in history. I tried to shoot a lot of pigeons with that little BB gun, but they were very safe up in the rafters of the closed livestock buildings.

Our great-aunts owned three small farms that were really the accumulated work of their parents and brothers. There was an eighty, a one-hundred-and-twenty, and a one-hundred-and-fifty-acre farm all now owned by the four remaining unmarried sisters. Family members lived on two farms and a hired hand on the third smaller farm. My aunts and the farms were a throwback to the diversified subsistence farming of earlier generations. They worked in a large garden, a small orchard, grapevines, as well as almost all types of livestock including dairy cows. That guaranteed you would eat well even in a bad crop year. Extended family gatherings for holidays were enormous often numbering over twenty-five adults and children running everywhere and assuring we had leftovers for a week.

I spent as many weekends and as much of my summer vacations as possible exploring every foot of every barn and shop on those farms. I did chores such as feeding chickens and pigs, and when I was tall enough, I graduated into shoveling cow manure out the windows in the dairy barn. Those piles out the window would later be scooped up and spread on the fields. That might not have really been my favorite chore. For some strange reason, I have always liked tart and sour foods so I would eat green apples before they were ready and chew on rhubarb even though my aunts would warn me I would get stomach aches and possibly even the runs. By the way, my aunts were right most of the time. I still love to suck on lemons and limes and luckily rhubarb and sour green apples are harder to come by for me these days.

I want to share with you a couple of my most specific memories from the farm. My uncle had bought a pony that really did not like being ridden. On an early spring day, when the pony had not been ridden all winter, my uncle saddled the pony, and when I got on, he gave it a smack on the butt. Big mistake, that pony ran straight at a woodpile and threw me right on top of the pile. I came out with several puncture wounds from nails and ended up going to the doctor for a fresh tetanus shot and some stitches. My Aunt Annie was so furious at my uncle; that pony was gone off the farm the next day. By twelve, I was big enough to help put up hay, but we had to move the old hay in the loft over to one side of the barn before putting up any new hay. I flipped over an old bale and exposed a hornet's nest. They attacked so fast; all I could do was run out the door of the loft hitting the hay wagon on the way down; and I took off running and swatting hornets all the way to the house howling like a banshee. I ended up with over a dozen stings and was once again run into town to see the doctor. Funny how many of the strongest and clearest memories often have a traumatic component.

Picking just a couple memories from grade school is a challenge. I went to the small Catholic school in town, and it was when nuns were still teaching in most of the grades. My personal problem was that my mother also taught at my school. Mom and Dad made it clear that we had to be exemplary students so as to not embarrass the family. In trouble at school, guaranteed in trouble at home. In second grade, my cousin was roughhousing on the playground and ran by and caught me in the mouth with an elbow and ripped the corner of my mouth open. A trip to the doctor for stitches closed my mouth up but left me with a bigger mouth according to my dad.

I have a vivid memory of the day President Kennedy was assassinated. All the nuns were crying, and we were sent home early. With my family being Catholic and back then Democrats, we were devastated; I was too young to really understand the implications of the assassination but sensed how deep the anguish was at school and home.

In the fifth grade, I had two dramatic issues with my teacher, which unfortunately was my mother. I got into a 'boy fights over girl' spat with one of my best friends, Gene, after school. We were teasing each other about having a crush on a girl, at twelve years old; we were just being silly. We both swung our books bags at each other; I however connected that caused Gene a very impressive black eye. At school, the next day, my mother saw Gene's shiner and called him up to the front of the class and demanded to know what happened. After some very intense cross-exam, Gene had to give me up. He tried to cover for me by saying he swung first and that we were just horsing around. Thanks, Gene, you saved me that day.

Fifth grade was rough because I was under constant surveillance. I say that because Mom said that I really had to be the best-behaved student in the class to prove she did not play favorites. That led to my worst day in all of grade school. I had to go to the bathroom bad and raised my hand, and when acknowledged, I asked to go to the bathroom. My mother said I could wait until the next break and continued with the lesson. After another ten to fifteen minutes in pure agony, I again raised my hand and asked to go to the bathroom. I was told to put my hand down that there were only a few minutes to the class break; unfortunately, I did not make it until break! I am not sure if having an accident in fifth grade is not the most embarrassing thing possible, but it sure must be right up there. My mother was so upset and ashamed that she had caused my accident that she snuck me home for a change of clothes. I can tell you that if I asked to go to the restroom the rest of the year, I was immediately dismissed from class.

My work ethic and working career started early. I learned early that it was nice to have your own money when you wanted to buy candy or go on a ride at the county fair, so I was always ready for a chance to earn money. I think I got a small allowance when growing up for my chores around the house, but I was always looking for ways to earn more. The first business venture I remember was suggested by my grandfather, who was a salesman and a real joker. He told me that if I collected real nice rocks and cleaned them up, I could sell them for good money. Since this was 1961 in a small Indiana town, no one bought rocks. I was way ahead of my time, just look at all the money spent on rock landscaping today.

Well, I took my little red wagon about one mile over to an old gravel pit and picked out a full wagon of great rocks. I hauled them home and washed them with our garden hose and dried them with one of my mom's dish towels. I really had a great wagon full of pretty rocks. In less than an hour, I was able to sell all my rocks to our neighbors for over two dollars. When I got home, Mom wanted to know about the mess by the outside hose and what on earth I had done to her towels. I proudly explained to my mother my successful rock selling business, and she just about went ballistic. I had to go back to every neighbor and return the money and let them keep my precious rocks. Apparently, she thought the neighbors would think we needed money and had sent their son out selling rocks. Really, she knew they just gave me money to be nice since I was cute back then, but I think my rocks were really nice.

Either way, my grandfather and I had to shut down the rock-selling business permanently. My first real chance to make money was when I turned eleven. In my town, you could get a paper route when you turned eleven, and I was waiting at the door of the newspaper office on my birthday. Our local paper was an afternoon paper delivered Monday through Friday, so as soon as school was over, we would ride our bikes or walk down to the office and get our papers. My route took me from downtown almost back to my home and generated a couple dollars a week, which was a windfall for a twelve-year-old in 1963. From that point on in my life, I was never without at least one job to generate my own income.

You may be thinking how I can claim that I am a pretty simple common average American. I am talking about a solid early childhood in small-town America. Well, there are thousands of other small towns each with hundreds of kids just like me all with similar experiences. We are all just part of what makes America. Plus, we are still early in my story. We will pick up later with our move to Chicago! No longer a small-town boy.

Chapter 2
Mom

Before I get too deep into my ruminations, I need to talk about one of the most critical influencers in my life, my mother. She was born in 1922 that puts her childhood right in the middle of the great depression. I think a lot of small-town America suffered less from the depression than some of the big cities and because relatives on my mom's side had three local farms; there was always enough to eat and often enough to help feed others. Growing up during the great depression must have taught lessons in life few of us younger people can understand today. Times have changed so much today; we have dozens of pieces of electronics: computers, tablets, TVs, and blue-toothed everything, while they may have had a radio to gather around in the evening. The concept of needing a three-car garage and an outside storage unit for storing possessions would have been beyond their comprehension. Their parents saw WWI, and they would save the world again with WWII. Try explaining that to today's spoiled generations.

My parents and grandparents were devout Catholics and deeply proud to be Americans. High moral character and a belief in hard work were ingrained deeply in all my extended family. Immigrating into the United States in the 1850s and 1860s, they left a legacy of wanting nothing more than to be Americans and pursue the American dream.

I really know very little about my mom's childhood except it was not an easy time, money was tight, and jobs were scarce. My mom and her generation had it tough and wanted little more than to make it really better for us in the next generation. She spent much of the war years at a Catholic women's teaching college getting a degree in English and her teaching certificate. My mother taught me her love of reading but not her love of grammar and spelling. I hated her constant correcting my punctuation and spelling, which I blame for my shortcomings in this area even today. Mom, I love you, but I still hate spelling and punctuation and being corrected. You would be proud to know that my wife has stepped in for you in this area.

I know very little about my mother's parents. Her father owned a small furniture store and worked as a mortician, while her mother was a teacher before getting married and becoming a full-time housewife. They each died in 1947 within a month of each other when my mom was only twenty-five. I know they had a deep religious faith and strong moral character, which was ingrained in my mother's core beliefs. The common threads I have found in all my extended family was their religion and absolutely no fear of hard work.

My parents married in our local Catholic church in 1948, and strangely, I just realized that I do not know if my dad even met my mother's parents. Being good Catholics, my parents did not waste much time in starting a family. Mom and Dad had five of us children in ten years and would have been more if not for a couple miscarriages. My uncle was an even better Catholic or at least more successful with eleven children. I can guarantee that as serious devout Catholics, birth control was simple; it did not exist.

My mother taught me many critical lessons in life. Of course, I taught her that when you have to go to the bathroom, you really have to go! Mom was stern and loving. She was so smart she knew how to make you think it was your idea when she wanted something done. When you were little and came running in the house crying from a fall, she could kiss the booboo and make sure it was fixed up before she sent you back out to play. When you were acting like you knew it all, she would know how to correct you. If I were out of line, she would remind me that Dad would be home in an hour and she would have to tell him. That was when parents were still allowed to give you a spanking. I rarely got out of line and to this day believe a lot more discipline would not hurt most of our young ones.

Just to give you a little window into how brilliant my mother was, let me share a couple of my favorite stories. My oldest sister was in a discussion with my mother about not attending Sunday mass. My sister believed her argument that she did not have to go to church; she could stay home and just say some prayers and that would mean just as much to God. Mom asked her if she received an invitation to a wedding would she just stay home and celebrate on her own. She explained that mass is a celebration of God with your Catholic community and you need to be there to get the most out of it. I am not sure it made much of an impression on my sister, but I loved it. I remember another time where Mom was talking on the phone to a fellow teacher on a school issue, and from the side of the conversation I could hear, it was all milk and honey. When Mom hung up, I was astonished because I knew that this individual was her least favorite person working at the school. I asked why she was so nice and agreeable, and she explained that even if she did not like someone, they would never know. She believed you keep all interactions with fellow human beings on a kind and professional level, and making enemies is never smart.

On another occasion, I remember one of my sisters asked Mom when she knew she loved Dad. She tried to explain that she was still learning what love is and how it grows with life's experiences together. When as parents, you are up all night with a seriously ill child, suffer together over a stillbirth, or face serious financial issues together you can grow in love. She wanted to make sure that we understand the difference between horny young sexual drives and infatuations and that they are dramatically different than deep love between two individuals. My mother believed you would not fully understand love until you held each other's hand in the final minutes of life.

When I reflect on her life, it looks to have been so much more difficult than my own. She was a child of the depression and as a young adult faced the horror of WWII. Her parents both died very young before she married. Then in her early forties, she started having hemorrhage in her eyes. They tried using lasers to burn the hemorrhaging to stop the bleeding, but each use cost permanent loss of vision at that spot. They were never able to totally control the vision deterioration, so she eventually had to quit teaching, which she dearly loved. My sister had severe medical problems that put her in home care. Mom and Dad struggled to maintain her at home but when Dad died, she finally had to move my sister into a nursing home. My sister was still only in her twenties. Then Mom was struck down by a central nervous system disease called pseudobulbar palsy. With all life's challenges thrown at my mother, I never heard her complaining. She loved all of us and life passionately.

Many of us are not lucky enough to have the perfect mother or for as long as I did.

Chapter 3
Dad

My memories of my father are hazy compared to my mother. They are all comfortable and warm but for some reason more generalized. I remember baseball, boy scouts, hunting, and roughhousing on the floor in the den with us kids all piling on Dad. But I have very few of the hard-crisp snapshot memories I have of others in my life. If I am not careful my description of Dad would seem like a characterization of the TV father of the 1950s. He was the provider and the disciplinarian, did the manly chores, and had his easy chair in front of the TV set. Most evenings, he would have a cocktail in his easy chair when he got home from work while Mom was preparing dinner. He really did make statements such as 'if you get in trouble at school, I better not hear about it because you will be in even more trouble with me'.

Dad was three years younger than my mother; his parents were second-generation Americans. His parents were also Catholic with his dad's parents from Ireland and his mother's having emigrated from Germany. The story was that my great-grandfather came over with eight brothers, and they dispersed when they hit American soil.

As good Catholics, they proliferated the family name all over the USA. Several times, I have met people with my last name, and they told me how their great-grandfathers had come over with eight brothers, making them distant previously unknown relatives! Dad was also a baby of the depression and WWII. He enlisted shortly after his eighteenth birthday and was overseas for four months when he was shot in the head by a sniper in the French theater.

Patching together what I could from Mom, and his brothers, the story was that he received a glancing blow in the eyebrow. The bullet took a chunk of bone out and popped his eye out of the socket. He collapsed in the mud and was left behind for dead during the advance. When they came back, they found him face down in the mud but alive. The mud had sealed the wound so that when he was brought to the field hospital, they cleaned away the mud and pushed the eye back into place. Miraculously, his sight was not affected, and except for the scar and no eyebrow, he had a full recovery. Dad like many WWII veterans would never talk about the war, but years later, he would tell me more about that particular day.

My dad was a natural athlete, and when he got home from the war, he went to play football at a college but found he could not wear a helmet. There was some nerve damage in his temple, and when he wore a helmet or even a tight hat, he was likely to get dizzy and pass out. I cannot find a single picture of my dad with any head covering on. He focused on fast-pitch softball after having to give up football, which in our area had semiprofessional corporation sponsored teams. My dad went to work for one of our local furniture factories and pitched for their traveling softball team. Mom was his best fan and saved newspaper clippings of a couple no-hitters and a perfect game he pitched. He definitely landed the job as much for his pitching as his strong back on the loading dock, but Dad ended up in top management spending his entire working career with just one company. Somewhere in his mid to late twenties, he started to have some issues with tripping and balance which years later was diagnosed as multiple sclerosis.

Unfortunately, that was not the end to Dad's back luck with his health. When he was forty-four, Dad sat up in bed and coughed up blood. X-rays showed he had a mass in his lung; the doctors had to remove two-thirds of his right lung, which was a walled-up mass of histoplasmosis, which is a fungal disease. If you grow up in the Midwest, you will probably test positive for histoplasmosis, but it is normally easily fought off with symptoms much like a common cold. In 1969, this was a very difficult operation, and Dad was in the intensive care unit for over a week. Later, the doctors said they almost lost him several times. This operation and multiple sclerosis really took their toll on Dad; he never got back to the strength and stamina he had up to that point. Amazingly, I never heard my dad complain no matter how difficult or painful his condition was.

My father was not a hugger or an outwardly affectionate person except with Mom. They were constantly showing affection for each other. With the five of us all fighting for attention or trying to avoid discipline, I am sure we were a handful for Dad to keep in line. But I know he really loved us, and occasionally, it really came out with something special. One of the most vivid memories I have of his doing something out of character showing his affection was when I was at a summer camp. My mom and I had set up to send each other cards while I was at summer camp. Mom made mine prestamped and numbered to make it easy for me to remember. It was fun to send and receive cards during my two weeks away from home. On the day before camp ended, I was called into the camp office for a special delivery letter. It was from my father, and he just wanted to say he was sorry he had not sent a note earlier, but he hoped I had had a great time, and he was looking forward to my getting home. That really meant a lot to me, and I kept that letter for years.

I can remember walking in the woods while my dad was hunting squirrels. He rarely had much luck when I was crashing through the woods next to him, but it was all about being out together. Another memory was a Knights of Columbus picnic with a fishing contest that we won with a little bluegill; I still have the picture of us with the winning fish. Some of my best times with Dad were when we commuted together; he would drop me at high school on the way to work, and later when he could not drive, I would drop him at work on my way to college. Again, most of these are just warm memories of a simple friendship. I knew as the oldest son I needed to step up and do my share around the house and the lawn. I knew how much Dad appreciated me working around the house and taking over the outside chores.

I have very few pictures of my mom or dad. Photography was a pretty expensive hobby, and neither of my parents was into taking pictures so what pictures there were we split up when my mom died. I have three special pictures of Dad, one with a close friend when they were leaders at a Boy Scout jamboree. He looked so young and athletic. I have one of him with my brother on the senior night of football and another with Mom and me at my college graduation. He beamed with pride for his boys in those two photographs; his love was so apparent.

One day, I picked up Dad from work at the corporate office, and he told me that he felt he needed to move back to our hometown. I was surprised because I knew both he and Mom really liked living in Chicago, but he explained that he felt with Mom losing her sight he wanted her settled back with the extended family around her for support. My mother later filled in some of the real backgrounds on Dad's decision to move back.

When Dad was shot on the battlefield in France, he said God talked to him and told him he would not die there; he would go home and raise a family and live to fifty. My dad never told this to anyone but my mother. He felt, when they married that she needed to know what God had told him, since it related to the time they would have together. So, when he was forty-eight and mom's vision was failing, he wanted her back where her brothers and their families were available for her when he died. Well, Dad was really close to being correct, shortly after he turned fifty-two, he again set up in bed and was coughing up blood. He had lung cancer, and it had metastasized to his liver. He died on 19 April, my brother's nineteenth birthday; years later, my invalid sister would die on 19 April also at the age of fifty-two.

Through all the difficulties, illness, pain, and suffering, I never heard my dad complain. He never questioned 'why me' in any way. He was more concerned for my sister or mother's health than his own. I believe that he felt that God had blessed him on that battlefield where so many died. If asked I think he would have answered much like Lou Gehrig did, 'that he was the luckiest man on the face of the earth'.

Chapter 4
Relocation

If you want to find a way to shake up a small-town boy, just relocate him inside the city limits of Chicago. That is just what we did shortly before my twelfth birthday. It may seem hard to believe but I did not really have much of an issue with moving, while my siblings seemed shell-shocked. I found friends quickly since baseball, basketball, and boys on bikes seem universal. I also went from one Catholic school to another and from one Boy Scout troop to another, easy and fun transitions. One difference was mom took a job at a different Catholic school than the one in which I was enrolled, so I had a little more leeway on my in-school behavior.

This was 1965 right in the middle of the civil rights movement but that really was not something I was paying any attention to at my age and being from a small rural town. We were a little naive moving into the city of Chicago. Our hometown had not had a murder in over thirty years, and with full employment, we really had little trouble in town. I would leave the house on my bike and be out all day with no concerns or with contact during the day with my parents. Racial turmoil over the next few years in Chicago made me more aware of my surroundings, but since I was never taught 'racism' growing up in a small town, I struggled to understand some of the issues.

When we relocated to Chicago, we rented a townhouse on Austin Ave near Lake Street where the elevated train made it easy to get downtown. I really was fascinated by the elevated train and would even take it downtown with a friend and walk out to Lake Michigan and fish for perch. Can you imagine parents today letting a thirteen- or fourteen-year-old take a cooler and fishing pole with a friend on the mass transit system to downtown Chicago, then walk out to a dock on the lake and fish all day? And in case you are not thinking back to that time, we did not have a cell phone so when we left the house you would not hear back from us until we got home late that evening.

We had a distant relative in Chicago who was a real estate agent and eventually we were able to find a nice house and move to Oak Park, the nearest west suburb of Chicago. This was a short six blocks to the Catholic school where my mother was teaching and still a reasonable commute to my dad's job. We were always a one-car family but with the new house, we also bought a second car. The house location was great for me; it was a nice residential neighborhood with lots of kids my age. We were only a couple blocks to transit lines so I could still go fishing at the lake or get around, and there was a great park just three blocks from our house. I could always find a basketball game in our alleys or a street hockey game. It was a great time and a fun neighborhood in which to be a teenager.

As cloudy or hazy as my early memories were of Rushville, my memories in Chicago are crisp and seem almost innumerable. I want to pick out some of the more interesting ones, which you might enjoy. These may paint me as a little hoodlum, but we mostly were good clean kids, just like most average American teenagers.

We had a public grade school a few blocks from our house that had a low flat roof easily climbed onto using the big rain drainpipes. One of your more daring endeavors would be for a couple of us to climb up to the roof and remove a skylight, then hang from the lip of the roof and drop to the floor inside. How we never hurt ourselves on that drop still amazes me. One of us would stay on the roof to put the skylight back then shimmy down the drainpipe, and we would open the door for them. We never did any vandalism, but we had some great hide and seek games with the whole run of the school. Eventually, they must have figured out we were getting into the school via the roof skylights because they put bars and padlocks on them. Probably saved us a broken leg!

We biked all over Oak Park and River Forest as teenagers. On one occasion, I biked with a friend out to a railroad track in Melrose Park. The train had to go very slowly over an overpass in that area, and we decided to try to jump on the train. The train really was not going much faster than a quick walking speed and was easy to jump on. But it quickly sped up after it crossed the bridge, and we realized we were in trouble! I decided to jump off and luckily, I thought to get low and kind of roll-off, a technique for a soft landing, and I was barely scratched. But my friend froze and just stood there, I ran along yelling for him to do like I did before it got to moving too fast. He finally just jumped up and out and landed extremely hard. I helped him up, and he was crying that he thought he had broken his arm. I did not know if he had or not since it looked straight to me. Of course, at that time, I did not know much about two bones in the forearm. Regardless of his pain, I convinced him we needed to get back to our bikes and get home as soon as possible, then figure out what to tell our parents. We agreed he could have hurt his arm in a simple bike crash.

I was not sure what happened when he got home, but he obliviously broke under questioning because he told his parents about our train ride. It was just my luck that they called my parents and told them the whole train story and how serious their son was injured, which did not seem fair since I was unhurt. That was the second maddest my dad ever was with me. As a side note, my dad was maddest at me the first time I used the F... word in our house, that occurrence led to a mouth wash out with a full bite out of a bar of soap!

During those awkward predating early teenage years, many of us hung out at a bowling alley a couple blocks from my house. We even bowled together in a youth league on Saturday mornings and in a youth summer league. I really did not like to bowl but the girls were a good enough reason to tolerate the league. In the back of the bowling alley was a bank of coin-operated telephones. Yes, we used payphones long before cell phones. As silly teenagers, we loved to call the girls and talk on the phone, which is still going on today just on cell phones and text messages. Somehow, someone found out you could stick a metal safety pin or needle through the cord of a payphone and touch it to metal and get a dial tone for a free phone call. We would spend hours and hours sticking a safety pin through the payphone cords and talking for free to our latest girlfriends. This must have become common knowledge because in later years, they used metal rapped cords on payphones. That sure would have messed up my early courting of the girls!

One of my first jobs after moving to Chicago was soliciting for subscriptions to the *Sun-Times* newspaper. Three to four of us were picked up by a team manager and went door to door to try to get people to sign up for the *Sun-Times* home delivery for which they would get a cheap gift, similar to those banks used to give someone for opening a new account. The best new sales results were apartment buildings where no solicitation was allowed. If you could get through the locked outside door it was easy selling because many of these people had never been approached for home delivery. Back then, many of the common doors to the apartments could easily be picked with a flexible piece of metal or a stiff plastic card. I was very successful selling these buildings once inside and knocking on individual apartments. The large apartment building strategy worked good enough to make me one of the top subscription sales boys, and I won a bike during one of the sales promotions. I do not think I ever told my dad about my entrance technique to enhance my sales numbers.

I think I will leave off here since I will pick up my stories later when discussing my high school education.

Chapter 5
Siblings

I did not grow up alone; two older sisters, a younger sister, and a little brother filled out the house. In Rushville, my three sisters shared a room, and my brother shared my room, with the same arrangement working at the townhouse in Chicago. However, when we moved to Oak Park, our basement had three bedrooms and a bathroom, which were claimed by my sisters. I however was again stuck sharing a room with my little brother. With us all being born in a short ten-year stretch, we were all still under the same roof when we arrived in Chicago, but at least, this was the first house where we had some real space and privacy. With my little brother being almost five years behind me, we really did not do a lot of activities together, except maybe when I was tickle tormenting him.

It is hard to write the story for my siblings since three of them are still making their own legacies. But for one of us, a very sad story is already over. My next older sister was really a funny and happy young lady who finished high school and was working as a waitress. She had moved into her own apartment when she had her first major flair-up of multiple sclerosis. Yes, my dad had MS also; there is a surprisingly high incidence of multiple members of family members having MS. The doctors had her on high doses of steroids that often helped patients but has side effects such as easy bruising, fluid retention, thin skin, slower wound healing, and other side effects. I can remember when she got kicked in the leg once and her skin split wide open with a large wound that was very difficult to heal.

One morning, when she was coming down icy steps at her apartment, she slipped and fell. She had internal injuries, then had blood clots go to her lungs causing multiple difficulties and lack of oxygen to the brain. She never fully recovered but had a couple good years living with my parents at home where we became closer friends. I would come home from college, and she would visit with me outside while I did chore around the house; however, later, she had additional complications that made her completely house, then bed-bound.

My parents did everything they could do to keep her at home but when my dad died, my mom eventually had to have her committed to a nursing home; she was in her mid-twenties when she entered a nursing home as a ward of the government. My sister spent the rest of her life in that nursing home and died on April 19 at the age of fifty-two, the exact day and age of my father's death.

Quickly, I will run through my other siblings, but since these writings are my ruminations, I will keep their involvement short and sweet. My oldest sister was married young at nineteen, divorced twice, and married a third time which stuck. Her third husband became a close friend of mine. I do not know if she ever learned, but I loaned Dad some money to cover her first wedding, which he quickly paid back. We have had more interaction over the years with my older sister than any of my other siblings since we ended up living in the Kansas City area for many years while raising our children.

My younger sister lives in my hometown and basically has most of her adult life. She even worked at the same furniture factory like my dad for several years. She was married divorced, remarried, and widowed. Her second husband committed suicide. She has two sons who also live near her and grandchildren she works hard to spoil. We have never lived close to each other since I left home, which is our main excuse for not being closer.

My little brother was just far enough behind me in an age that we never did much together. I pretty much moved out my last two years of college, and he was still in high school back in my hometown. It may be strange, but I think of myself as much more as from Chicago than Rushville. While my brother returned in time for high school and had some great friends from Rushville, which he keeps in touch with even today. So, he is more connected to Rushville than I am. There is really no one in Rushville except for my sister I have any contact with anymore.

All my mom's generation is gone, and even though my uncle's family is enormous and mainly all still in Rushville, I have no real contact with them. My brother is happily married with two grown sons, and now, his first grandchild. Over the years we were not the best at keeping in touch, but we have grown closer over the years, and I even suffer a game or two of golf with him each year. Golf is the only sport he beats me at easily and at our age basketball would have to be at best a game of horse.

My parents and their parents rarely moved far from their family and had deep local roots. That is of course after they made it over from Europe and dug those roots. Their closeness both here and for generations in Europe was necessary to survive. My generation seems to be one of the first in America that moved often and everywhere. During my career, companies used to move managers frequently in their careers, this practice has slowed down somewhat because of the costs of relocation. With our career mobility and extreme distance from home, we lost some of the best of the close family ties and family-based activities of previous generations. Looking back, I would have enjoyed having more time with my parents and siblings. But life is fast, and I was in a hurry. Going forward, I think I need to reach out and create some new memories with my siblings before it is too late.

Chapter 6
High School

I went to an all-boys Catholic high school in Chicago, run by Christian Brothers. Discipline was extreme by today's standards, but if you were going to pay for a private school, you expected an education. I picked this school over a closer all-boys Catholic high school in Oak Park or the local public high school. I picked the Chicago school because some of the friends I had from my old neighborhood were going there, and the Oak Park guys I knew were a little stuck up. Since private high school was a significant cost for us, I agreed to pay part of the tuition. It also was on the way to my fathers' work so I could ride with him most of the time.

High school holds a lot of very vivid memories, and almost all of them are good. I made some good friends, wrestled for the first couple of years, and got good grades. After my sophomore year, I stopped wrestling for more time to work part-time jobs, and the money was nice to have if you wanted to go out with friends or to date. I bussed tables at a high-end restaurant and worked at Jack-in-the-box, plus odd jobs such as mowing and painting. I have always liked to earn and have my own money, and this drive increased with new high school activities.

Time seemed to fly. I would ride to school with Dad, try to stay out of trouble with the Christian Brothers, ride home with Dad, part-time job, then homework. I took advanced classes in the sciences which were my favorite classes. I had one teacher that had five master's degrees, one in education and the others in sciences. He never stopped going to school while teaching and was so enthusiastic he made chemistry or biology fun. Most of my teachers were lay teachers, but I had several Christian Brothers and one of them was really a masochist. You learned to never misbehave in his class; he really did use a ruler to smack kids around. School discipline in the 1960s was quite different from today; I am sure this brother would not have lasted a semester anywhere else than in a Christian Brothers boys high school. Let me help you understand the discipline at our school. In junior year, I was sitting in the back of a class when a student sitting across from me asked what the teacher had said; while answering him, I was ripped out of my chair, pulled out into the hallway, and slapped across the face. The school disciplinarian, who I think was also a masochist, did not even give me a chance to say anything in my defense, he just yelled at me that 'I do not talk in class unless called upon'.

Even setting aside the strict discipline in high school, it was not without a couple strange or difficult situations. We had an indoor pool at our high school, which was rare at the time, and believe it or not we had all our gym swimming classes in the nude. Yes, this is not a joke, and when you are an underdeveloped pre-puberty male in class with some Italian friends already shaving, embarrassed is not even close to a strong enough word. Add to that that I had never really learned to swim more than to thrash myself over to the side of the pool if I jumped in, obviously I despised this class. Luckily, you only had to do a semester of swim, I never went in that pool the rest of my four years there. The only decent thing that came out of the class is I could swim the length of the pool by the end of the class.

Today, people talk about bullies like it is the end of the world. My mom and dad taught me to ignore most idiots or to walk away, but only so far. I had some good friends, but with my class load and my working, I was not the social butterfly. But for some reason, I had one kid in homeroom that decided he liked agitating me. I really let it slide until junior year when he spat on me. Even a sweet nonviolent kid like me felt that was the tipping point. I said I would see him after class in the alley behind our football practice field where all the school fights were staged.

Now, he was the tight end on the football team, and I wrestled in the one eighteen-weight class. So, a six-foot-two guy against five-foot-six runt was not a wise choice for me. Then of course word got around school that there was going to be a fight. One of the gym teachers heard about the fight and tried to have us box under his direction, which was an allowed way to settle things. This assured for some strange reason you would not be suspended from school. I thought that was an even worse idea with my opponent's long reach, so the alley fight was on.

I remember I got hit several times but got inside his reach and attached myself around his neck and flailed away until pulled off by a policeman. In the melee of the police breaking up everyone, I was able to walk off before they again grabbed me. I tried to plead ignorance, but the cop pointed out my black eye and bloody shirt as proof I had been one of the participants. They took us back to the school office and left us with the school principal. I got a short suspension which included not being able to attend the junior prom while on probation. To be honest, I would not have gone to the dance anyway with my two black eyes. Believe it or not, I gave a little more than I got in the fight and that was the end of any issues I had with that bully, but I would not say we ever became friends.

You might think that going to an all-boys Catholic high school might retard your social life with the other sex, but you would be wrong. We had an all-girls Catholic high school less than six blocks away and there was another all-girls Catholic high school just a couple miles straight west of our school. I think keeping us separate in all-boys and all-girls' schools made for even more repressed hormones. The sidewalks and roadways were very busy between our schools once the last bell rang. I think I ended up dating girls from at least four different all-girls Catholic high schools in Chicago.

I really had a nice group of friends in high school and a group of us also went on to the same college. Several of the guys were in a good local rock and roll band and when I was not working, I was pretty much heading out to anywhere they were playing. They did a lot of high school sock hops and some club gigs. A large group of us loved

went, she still cried at the ending. My parents really liked her, but her dad did not like me. I was in a period where I thought a lot of myself and was still checking out the whole world of dating. I screwed up playing around down at the beach with some other girls and she broke up with me. Her dad made sure we did not get back together.

I bounced around and dated a few different girls but nothing serious. Even when I started dating my current wife it seemed a little more casual and progressed in a slower and simpler manner. Since we had known each other from our common friends it sometimes seemed like more of a group hangout situation as opposed to a date. I might have said something like 'do you want to go to where the bands playing this weekend' knowing all our friends would be there. Asking like that is less risky in case you are worried about rejection. This led to six years of dating even with my relocation and our multiple colleges. I think growing as friends through the years and sharing so much together in each other's lives made for a super foundation for a lasting marriage. Of course, I have to share a couple dating stories with you that my wife hates!

We started dating between my first and second years in college. I was eighteen, and I think we had our first date shortly after her sixteenth birthday. A lot of our dating was just hanging around, watching TV, and playing cards with her sister. We went to one of my fraternity parties which may have allowed some underage drinking and on the way to drop her at home she fell asleep, and I got stopped by the police for going the wrong way on a one-way street. I have no idea how I escaped with only a ticket since we had both drank a few beers. Rarely has getting a traffic ticket felt like such a lucky day.

After my second year of college, my family relocated back to Rushville, and I transferred to a college in Indianapolis. While separated, that first year, my girlfriend and I wrote hundreds of letters and cards, and I drove up to Chicago every chance I got. Letter and card writing as a form of communication have sadly been replaced with texting, but this was long before the cell phone. The next year we were reunited when she enrolled at the same college, this was when we probably realized we were seriously committed, and I was not escaping so easily.

My future wife finished her nursing degree while I went on to finish my master's at a university an hour down the road. I then headed out to the University of Oklahoma to work on my PhD. After she graduated, she took a job at Rushville Hospital three blocks from my mom's house. I came home from Oklahoma at Thanksgivings and saw that my girlfriend was living at my mom's house. That pretty much said it was time for us to get married. I guess I did a lot of dating but most of it was six years with the same wonderful girl.

Chapter 8
College

College included some dramatic changes just as disruptive as my move from Rushville to Chicago and back again. I spent my first two years at a large inter-city University as a full-time commuter, then transferred to a small college back in Indianapolis living on campus. In my first two years, I joined a fraternity, worked like mad on a couple part-time jobs, and did not focus like I should have on classes. The last two years, I lived on campus, focused on grades, and worked only weekends, summer, and winter vacations. My college experience was like two different lives.

I was one of the last years for the Vietnam war draft, and I had a high enough number that there was little chance of being drafted so I could focus on school. I was not exactly a hippy or anti-war activist, although my hair was a little long. With my dad having been in WWII in Patton's army I would have gone if drafted. I had too many issues to help with at home with Mom and Dad's illnesses to think about enlisting.

Being in college in the early 1970s I did go through my own bit of introspective about how my generation was going to change the world. I of course read books such as *The Prophet* and *Jonathan Livingston Seagull* and wrote my own poems. I did one short booklet of prose which I thought was pretty good, I would love to look at it today, but it was destroyed in a basement flood years ago. I wonder what I would think of poems today if I could read them.

I was a biology major thinking I would like to go to medical school. I believed I would specialize in research and cures for diseases such as multiple sclerosis and histoplasmosis, which had struck my family members. Even though my major was Biology I took a lot of courses on religion and arts which would feed what I perceived as my introspective side and help change the world. I took courses such as *Reflections on Man*, *Reflections on God*, *Art Forms Non-Western-World*, *Afro-American History from 1860*, *Expository Writing*, and *Man in his Community*. From this partial list, you can see how much of a deep thinker I truly thought I was. Between classes, I hung out at our fraternity table in the cafeteria or worked on my table tennis or foosball skills.

I was working the night part-time swing shift at UPS in downtown Chicago. You would start at nine pm and work until finished with the day's parcel sorting around two am. I was lucky to be in bed by three am most days. One of my course requirements was *Statistics*, and it only fit in my schedule at the eight am slot. I was lucky I did not end up falling asleep behind the wheel many times that semester on my way home from work or on my way to school. I sat in the back of the class and often fell asleep. One day the teacher threw an eraser at me and hit me in the head because he was fed up with me falling asleep. I fought through the semester and aced the tests and was shocked when I got a D. I went straight to the dean for a grade resolution meeting. At the meeting, the professor tried to say that class participation was fifty percent of the grade, and I failed that component with my constant falling asleep. I told the dean my work schedule and reviewed my test scores and he sided with me and the grade was raised to a B. I told the teacher that I hoped I would run into him somewhere during the summer so we could have a private discussion. That was as close as I ever came to actually want to punch a teacher.

The first two years went by in a blur between commuting with my dad, classwork, two part-time jobs, and trying to keep up with my social life which included the fraternity activities. The final two years at the small college in Indianapolis were totally different. I had won two small scholarships and had saved enough to live on campus and to only work weekends and holidays during the school year. That allowed me to focus a lot more on school, and I went from a B minus student to a B plus student in the final two years. I could and should have done better than that, but I never pushed myself as much as I should have, plus my first semester living in a dorm was a nightmare. My roommate was an older Vietnam veteran back on the school bill, but he was a bad drunk. At twenty years old, I really did not know how to handle him and would have moved off campus, but they found me a small single room at term break. A single room really was the key to my improving my grades and suited my personality.

My primary part-time job was now just weekends, and it was being a night watchman at a factory in my hometown about an hour from school. My uncle ran the crew of watchmen and put me on the three to eleven weekend shifts whenever I wanted. That was really a great job to get in a lot of studying, all you did was make the rounds of the plant once per hour which took about ten minutes and you could study the rest of the time. I picked up some extra work during the holidays, so I always had enough money to get by on my own. My parents were just an hour away, but it was great to be out on my own while still close enough to help them out around the house.

My first year in Indianapolis at college was the era of streaking. I was at a McDonald's when a group of four people streaked the restaurant, two young women and two men. I really did not mind the activity since both the women looked quite athletic. However, when a rather rambunctious freshman streaked our college library it created quite an issue. Did I mention this was a small Catholic college with some teaching nuns? Since the streaker had a full ski mask on, you could not prove who had done the dirty deed, but most of us in the men's dorm knew. Word gets around, and eventually, the culprit was called to the deans' office and was compelled to confess, he was promised no serious actions would be taken if he would just confess, so he eventually admitted to being the streaker. He was immediately expelled which I thought was unfair and not too religiously forgiving. That assured me that I would not be convinced to try any streaking on campus!

In my senior year, my girlfriend arrived on campus. I had worked a full-time job up in Chicago over the summer, so we pretty much got to campus together. I remember on the freshman day one of her soon-to-be best friends was walking around in one flat shoe and one high heel shoe, which on a little five-foot-nothing girl looked painful. I stopped her and she said a sophomore in her dorm told her to do it as part of one of those silly freshman games. I said to stop it immediately, and as a senior, my directive overruled a sophomore. I told her if she had any problems in her dorm to tell the idiots that hazed her to call me. I had no idea that would be my girlfriend's suitemate and become her best friend for all four years.

I really had a great senior year both in the classroom and being a kind of big brother for my girlfriend and her new friends and suitemates. I think they liked having a senior as kind of their guardian. I even joined the new soccer club team as the goalie and had a great time. Most of the college soccer programs for men back then were clubs with some college money to support our activities. We were self-coached but pretty good since we had a large contingent of foreign exchange students. We even played the Norte Dame club which was the first time I played as a goalie on artificial turf. I skinned up my knees and elbows with carpet burns, and I learned going forward to have a long sleeve goalie shirt and goalie pants on all future artificial fields. Life was good, grades were better, and I landed a fellowship for grad school.

Chapter 9
Grad School

I had landed a teaching fellowship that covered virtually all my direct school costs. In my mind with the fellowship, I needed to treat grad school like a job. It was time to really focus on the grades. With an undergraduate degree in Biology, I had picked a graduate program in Life Sciences at a large university in Indiana, an hour from Indianapolis. I decided that I was not going to settle for anything, but A's, and I did; I pulled off a perfect 4.0 GPA in grad school. I felt that this was a focused field of study that I had picked so there was no excuse to not like the classes and to excel. Again, I felt I had to look at this as a full-time job where I owed myself better results than I had achieved in undergraduate school.

Grad school put me a short hour over to my old college and my girlfriend and still only two hours to my parents, both easy commutes for social activities and to help at home on weekends. I had a great summer job during the summer and could still get some weekend shifts as a night watchman so spending money was not a problem.

This was the first non-Catholic institution I had ever attended. I attended three Catholic grade schools, a

Catholic high school, and two Catholic colleges. That almost makes you an honorary priest; however, I had not exactly lived the priestly life, and I surely loved the opposite sex. Trust me I never considered joining any order of the church. A much larger university with no religious affiliation was a bit of a culture shock and made it easy to miss Sunday mass except when visiting my parents.

As busy as I was with classes and my teaching assistantship duties, I still seemed to have more time available than ever before. I started working out more in the gym and worked in a pickup basketball game several times a week. I even got on with a local softball team. Because I always was goal-oriented, I decided that just working out was not enough, so I trained in Olympic and powerlifting with the intent to compete. I mainly trained with a new friend in the same science department who was a rower when an undergraduate out east. We hit the weight room and worked in long runs together, I hated to run, and he hated heavyweights, so we made a good pair. If I wanted to repeat two years of my life just for fun these would be near the top.

I had traded in my used Vega for a brand-new Vega which I ordered from the factory. Not many people have a soft spot for a Chevy Vega, but I owned two and they did right by me, and with a steady girl I did not need a 'chick' car. I lived in the coed graduate student dorm just a couple blocks from the science building and next to the field house, so my little Vega did not move much during the week. That first winter we had a record cold snap that still stands forty-five years later. We were projected to go somewhere between twenty-seven to thirty below zero in Terre Haute, Indiana. I was so concerned for my new Vega, which had an aluminum block and might not handle the extreme cold. So not knowing better or willing to take a chance. I went out every two hours from around eight pm until eight am and started and ran the car for about ten minutes. The next morning, I think I ended jumping five or six cars that would not start, obviously they were not up all night like I was.

In graduate school, I lived in a coed dorm reserved for graduate students only. A coed dorm was new to me at the time they sure were not found at the Catholic college I had attended. Even in this dorm, the switchboard for phone calls was closed at midnight until six am. Remember this was 1976, no one had cell phones. So, when my room phone rang through one morning around three am I knew something was wrong. Only emergency calls were put through by security that early. It was my mom; my father had just died. My mom asked if I could drive over and tell my brother in person. She did not feel she could handle calling him since it was 19 April his nineteenth birthday. He was a freshman at college a couple hours away from me. When I showed up at his dorm, he thought I had come over to visit since it was his birthday, but he quickly realized something was up. We had not really kept him up on how sick Dad was since we thought Dad had more time, but cancer had other plans. That was by far the most difficult assignment my mom had ever dropped on me, but I understand how she just could not have made that phone call to him. Looking back, I am glad I was able to be there, it made it a litter easier for each of us to head home together.

I finished up all my course work and defended my master's thesis and then had to make some critical decisions. With a master's and my 4.0 GPA I could probably now get into medical school, but I had decided that was not the direction that interested me anymore. The real disease research was more done by specialized PhD's running research programs. So, I applied for and was granted a full fellowship at the University of Oklahoma, I was going to study Medical Mycology. Time for another big change!

Chapter 10
Marriage

I am trying to work in somewhat of chronological order here, and my marriage was the next big step in my rather simple, average American life. But this will really be about some of our early years together. You will also get insights into our union in many of my aligned topic discussions. Plus, our story is still being written even after six years of dating and almost forty-two years of blissful marriage. I guess you could try to argue that I cannot be a very average guy with such a long marriage, but you need to know statistics and a bell curve, and you would see we fall well within the curve.

I finished my master's and went out to Oklahoma University to work on a PhD in Medical Mycology which turned into a disaster. Medical Mycology studies fungus diseases such as histoplasmosis, an obvious interest I had for many years. Immediately upon arrival, I was notified by the dean that the person I had come to study under had suddenly taken a job at the National Institute of Health. He assured me my fellowship was secure but I would have to pick another professor and discipline to pursue since they did not know if or when they would fill a new Mycology position. I spent two months looking at the other professors and areas of study and decided I had had enough schooling. While home at Thanksgiving I answered an ad for a QA supervisor at a dairy processing plant in Cincinnati and got the job. It was a perfect fit because I had spent four years working part-time and summers in a dairy lab in the Chicago area. I went back to Oklahoma packed up my things, resigned my fellowship, and headed to Rushville. I have often been asked if I regretted not finishing my PhD and the answer is no. The only thing I enjoyed in Oklahoma was meeting some serious powerlifters in a club at the university where I had a couple great months of training. I even competed in a two-man dead lift with a new friend, as a team we pulled almost a thousand-pound dead-lift!

When I arrived back in Rushville, my girlfriend was living with my mom. Since Mom had been living alone, there was plenty of room in the house. Her job was only a couple blocks from our house so it was a great arrangement. My new job at the dairy processing plant was about seventy miles, too far for a daily commute but I had an aunt and uncle near Cincinnati who were also empty nesters, so they put me up during the weekdays. My girlfriend paid rent to my mom, which unknowing my mother put into an account, and handed the money back to us at the wedding. With us both working and pretty much living at my mom's house it sure seemed a good time to get engaged. Being the pure romantic I am my proposal may have fallen a little short of most normal standards. I was dropping my girlfriend off for a weekend night shift at the hospital three blocks away. I could not let her walk being the chivalrous guy I was. As she got out of the car, I said something like 'it seemed like we out to get married'. I think I had to stop back later to make sure and reinforce that I was serious. The next day we went down and picked out a ring at a small jewelry store whose owner had been one of my fathers' best friends. Yes, we were officially engaged after over five years of dating, that girl sure had some patience with me.

We got married 11 November 1978; that is veterans' day and is also right around the opening day of deer hunting season which has caused a lot of consternation over the years. Lucky, we had been able to work around deer hunting conflicts with most of the compromise on her side, meaning a trip or something special before or after my hunting adventures. One of the smart things about marrying a nurse is she will almost always find a great job wherever you may end up living. She found a job immediately in the Cincinnati area, and we rented an apartment above a garage, that really was quaint but had no insulation and burned through fuel oil like crazy in the winter, which leads to a lot of cuddling that first year just to keep from freezing.

Marriage too is not a short race like a five- or ten-kilometer road race. Heck, it is not even like a half marathon. You can easily run the short races with little work and the half marathon maybe with only some training. But a long marriage is like a marathon it takes serious dedication and my wife had to patiently train me. In fact, I think I am now into the ultra-marathon persistence level of marriage with forty-two years under my belt. It takes a serious commitment, by two people to make it work. Remember you take wedding vows! I cannot say we never had some rough times especially when you see my work career which dragged my wife back and forth across the United States.

I remember one night we were living outside Indianapolis and had been out for the night. On the way home, we got into some argument that turned a little spicier than normal. I am sure I was the one out of line, but I could be stubborn sometimes back then. When we got home, we put the kids to bed, and I grabbed a pillow and went downstairs to sleep on the couch. Maybe twenty or thirty minutes later my wife came down the stairs and yelled at me that if I were going to stay on the couch, I could just call a lawyer in the morning. I thought about that for a few minutes and headed up to bed. That was probably as close to getting into trouble as I needed. She probably did not mean she would divorce me if I stayed on the sofa, but I figured why test her.

I remember rather vividly when I was around seven the 'grownups' were having hushed discussions at a holiday gathering. My father's sister was getting divorced. Do you realize how traumatic that was for a Catholic family in 1960? Although more common today (both my sisters are divorced and remarried) it is still a struggle for all involved. But even the Catholic Church realizes that not all marriages are truly a complete union as described in the bible which says, "And the two shall become one flesh; so then they are no longer two, but one flesh." Because of this, they have a process called annulment to dissolve marriages that were never really a union of spirits. No one should stay in a bad or abusive marriage, but divorce should be a last resort. Luckily, my wife is still putting up with my poor humor and idiosyncrasies.

All the time I had dated and when we were engaged, I said I did not want to have children. That was probably just my self-centered youth talking but she never argued and clearly knew how I felt about having children. I am not sure where the no children idea had gotten into my head coming from good Catholic stock. Eventually, I just grew up a little over the next couple years, and one day, I told her I thought I wanted children. If I remember correctly, she was so happy that she cried. She had married me knowing she wanted children and that I said I did not, but she married me and never pushed the subject once. Our daughters were not accidents, they were planned down to the week. I am glad I matured in our marriage and that we had children because for me life would have been so much less fulfilling without our children.

A good marriage really is the truest form of a partnership. Corny as it may sound, if you can try to set aside your own selfishness and think of your partner first, it gets ridiculously easy. It is even easier if she is also thinking of you first. However, setting aside your own selfishness is ridiculously difficult for most individuals. We are really becoming more self-centered every generation. With less need for subsistence living like our ancestors only a couple generations ago, we waste our leisure time in self-absorbing activities. A good marriage is hard work, and we are becoming lazy.

So we were just another average American family, married husband and wife with two children. It takes a lot of work, laughs, and even many tears, but marriage can be well worth the effort. Our dating and first few years of marriage were full of work and fun activities. We put some money in the bank and continue discovering a lot about each other. The next phase of marriage was to squeeze parenting in while keeping our careers going. Then before you can believe, you are empty nesters. As empty nesters, you often can really start putting money away for retirement. Now I guess we slow down and enjoy grandchildren, or maybe we get even crazier, that part of the story is still being written.

Chapter 11
Children

If you have children, you know that trying to describe how great they are to others is a small challenge. We had two beautiful daughters, and their list of accomplishments is extensive. Now, I know that may sound like a very proud father, and you would be right. So, it will be a struggle to keep this chapter short and succinct, without sounding like a pompous parent.

Both my daughters were born in Fresno, California. Then we made the decision we wanted to get back to the Midwest to be closer to family and to give them what I felt was a good old-fashioned Midwestern upbringing. My father had died, and Mom was limited with her diminished eyesight so it was important to us that she could spend some time with her granddaughters.

Since my job was outside sales the responsibility to handle day to day raising of the girls fell disproportionally on my wife. Looking back, I am not sure how she could get them up, dressed, fed, and then off to daycare by herself. She would then work her full shift at the hospital, pick up the girls, and once home deliver the attention they required while I was in a hotel somewhere. Hands down she had the tougher job the first few years. I later moved into the corporate office and traveled less so I could pick up more of a load of parenting.

With our educations, we were committed from day one to work on early education with them at home and then we enrolled them in a Montessori school followed by a private Catholic grade school. I think it paid off with a rich experience and a solid foundation.

I remember I came home from a business trip and my wife proudly announced that I was the coach of my youngest daughter's soccer team. Bewildered, I asked how that happened. The story goes that this was a fun league and the parents were the coaches and since I had played soccer in college I got elected. I tried to duck it because with my travel schedule I could not do practices, but they pretty much only did activities at this level of fun soccer on weekends, so I was hooked. Coaching my daughter then both daughter's soccer teams became one of the true joys of my life. I adjusted my schedule, and over the next twelve years, I coached two and even three girls' soccer teams with my daughters and many of their friends. I decided to do it right and went through multiple levels of coaching classes culminating in getting my national D coaching license. I heard that many men would have competitive issues and could not coach their own daughters, but we never had any problems. I loved coaching them and they loved playing for our teams. I guess we did pretty well because they both played in college on scholarships.

I also got to add basketball coaching to my resume with my youngest daughter, while my wife worked with my oldest daughters' grade school basketball team. Although all the teams we worked with including, soccer and basketball were very successful; I think we always kept the focus on learning skills and having fun. I wish I could say this for all the parents and other coaches we knew, they were always more of a challenge to control than the kids.

The girls really knew when they liked a sport or an activity. They at one time or another tried volleyball, soccer, softball, basketball, gymnastics, tennis, cross country, singing class, and a few more I am sure I am missing. One day, my younger one came to us and announced she wanted to quit gymnastics. When asked why, she stated she had gotten to practice early and did all her stretching. When the teacher arrived, she told them to stretch and my daughter said she did, but the teacher did not believe her and said do it again. She was not happy that the teacher did not believe her and that was enough to turn her off on the class and gymnastics. I could guarantee you if she said she had stretched, she did!

Both girls did great with their grades but to maintain correct focus on school over sports I told them they could participate in as many activities as they wanted but if they got a B they lost a sport, the second B would lose another sport! When my oldest daughter graduated high school with a perfect 4.0, she asked me would she really have had to lose a sport with a B grade. I simply replied she would never need to know the answer to that question. My younger daughter repeated the 4.0 feat with even more sports and outside activities.

If you are a parent, there are two things I think you will need to be prepared for. At some time, boundaries will be tested. Second, you will become stupid compared to their vast knowledge. The boundaries will get tested often more than once and sometimes constantly. You will suddenly get stupid while they are teenagers and may stay that way into old age. Children just cannot conceive of you having been young once and just as brilliant as a teenager as they now are. On one occasion, both daughters were at a party with another pair of sisters of the same ages. The younger daughter called and asked if she could stay over at the friend's house, which I agreed to but said she still had an earlier curfew. Their friends were a little wilder than my daughters, and I guessed this was a ploy for all of them to stay out late. So, at the time she should have been back at their house I drove over and waited, and waited, and waited outside their house on the street. She finally arrived way after curfew. I simply had her get in the car, and we drove home in silence. We never discussed it much, but she needed to know as parents we were not stupid and lying was not acceptable.

I really cannot imagine what life would have been like if we did not have our two daughters. They have fulfilled our lives and really what is a legacy other than the children you raise. There were times when they were a challenge to balance with work and any personal time but worth every second of the effort. You really build the foundation with them early, and hopefully, when they get to high school and college, their work ethic and moral base sustain them. As parents we want them to go even farther than we have. We stood on our parents' shoulders, and we want them to stand on ours and reach for even better. I think that virtually, all parents feel the same way about their children.

Chapter 12
Work

I will tell you right now that I believe in the dignity of work. For me there is nothing better than the feeling of a job done well, even simple things such as mowing a lawn or painting a room are rewarding. Hard honest work builds the soul and strengthens the backbone. The following is a list of jobs I have had in my life so far that I will admit to.

My work history:

- Selling rocks in my neighborhood
- Newspaper boy
- Selling newspaper subscriptions
- Busboy at the restaurant banquet hall
- Jack-in-the-Box restaurant
- UPS swing shift at night
- Hill farm dairy lab technician, worked after school, holidays, and summers for four years.
- Night watchman on weekends
- 7UP night shift lab tech

- Bartending at Knights of Columbus restaurant, hall, and bowling alley
- Quality Control French Bower Dairy
- Sanitation supervisor at a distillery
- Supervisor at Kroger bakery
- QC lab supervisor chemical/food packaging plant
- Chemical sanitation outside sales
- QC for ice cream production
- Regional sales specialist chemical sanitation
- Switched to different Chemical Sales organization
- Returned to previous sales organization after an acquisition
- VP of a national chemical sales organization
- Started independent consulting LLC
- Returned as president of previous chemical sales organization
- Contracted to be interim-president of a chemical company – the owner had a stroke
- Joined Food Sanitation Consulting organization
- VP of a new chemical sanitation organization
- Started a new food sanitation consulting group with a partner
- VP of Americas for global Ag equipment manufacture
- Owned golf course
- Retired investor and board member chemical manufacturer

I did almost any job to make a buck during high school and college. Not listed above is bailing hay, furniture moving, painting neighbor's house, mowing lawns, or babysitting. One of my most lucrative part-time jobs if you want to look at it as a job was running a trap line on weekends and winter holidays for fur, I made enough one winter to pay for half a year of college tuition.

If you look at the above list, you might think I could not hold a job. However, that would be far from the truth. The first ten are all the jobs I had as a youth or later to get through all my years of high school and college. Over thirty years of my career were with three companies. There were two organizations I worked for that recruited me back multiple times. I never lost a job, and I always had a new challenge lined up before I left an organization. My relationships with every employer or consulting customer were excellent because I always gave over one hundred percent. I believed that at the end of each day you need to have earned that day's salary.

I enjoyed most all the jobs I have had but some were more rewarding. When consulting, I often worked on quality control and environmental sanitation issues in food and beverage organizations. When you could help them solve issues and assure a safer food supply, it is rewarding. I also loved chemical sales where I again approached problem-solving chemical sanitation issues with my clients. To me, being a sales representative was a competition, and I hated to lose. When hiring salespersons, I found that often the most successful were very competitive people that had played sports. When in management roles, I often found myself frustrated with the office work and could not wait until I could get out and be with my customers. I found leading from the field more effective than leading from my desk.

I have always tried to explain to people that worked for me the value of earning your wages every single day. Imagine you needed to take money out of your own pocket or savings account to pay someone for their day's work. People rarely personalize how it would feel to have to take money out of their own pocket to pay someone for poor or sloppy work. It may seem ok to screw off when some big rich corporation is paying you but, would pay for poor work performance from your personal savings?

I have a work philosophy that would have a dramatic effect on our whole social system if instilled into the populous. For all time of humanity, we have had to work as part of our personal survival. Whether as a prehistoric hunter-gatherer or a farmer or working in a factory you worked to live. Work is a barter system; we have not been completely independent since prehistoric times and even then, you may have traded an animal hide for a new spear. I only have so many hours of life I can work or barter. I may choose to work harder than anyone else around me so I may have accumulated more money or possessions. Since I live in a complex society, I can trade my money. That money was earned by working, which is hours of my life traded for value. I may want to pay for police, fire departments, and schools while I have school-age children. For those services, I am fundamentally trading working hours of my life. When an oppressive government, a dictator, or a communist system comes in and under the threat of a gun confiscates my money or possessions is that not another form of slavery? They are taking hours of my working life against my will.

We all have so many hours of work available and with my hours shouldn't I have the God-given freedom to spend those hours or dollars as I choose? Why should any oppressive system imposed by man have the right to take my freedoms or the hours available of my life? Imagine some official showing up with a gun at your house today and telling you that you are going to clean someone else's house today for six hours then you can do your own work after that. When I ask why, they do not clean their own house he may say that they are lazy so I should do it for them! You are taking hours of my life at the threat of force, what for the good of society? Redistributing hours of my life because I am a hard worker and others are not! It should be my choice what I do with my hours of life and the dollars I earn.

I gladly buy the services or contribute to the items I want and use. I drive a car so I would contribute to roads. I use city services, so I need to pay for those services. Charity is a personal choice, and I should not have my life's hours confiscated for someone else to decide who should have my charity. When my children are school age, I should pay for their education but at a place of my choosing. If I can find them a great school for five thousand a year, why should the government confiscate my life's hours for an expensive inferior education? The big government inner-city schools spend $25,000 to $30,000 per student per year for terrible schools. They are run for the benefit of the teachers unions not for the good of the students and taxpayers. Why am I paying for other children's educations once I have no children in school? You are stealing my life hours available to work or barter in many ways and areas that infringe on my freedom. We are slaves or indentured servants to a government that wastes money. The elected officials think the government makes money; no, it only confiscates our money. They have no concept of reaching into their own personal pockets or spending their life hours to pay for services they so freely give away. The government has no hours of work available they can only steal hours of our life.

In general, for tens of thousands of years if you wanted to eat, you worked. Nothing wrong with that. There is dignity in work. But also, for tens of thousands of years, someone has wanted to dominate you to work so they could eat or have leisure. I can agree to organize around a minimal system of government for national defense and foreign affairs, but most everything else should be a local system of buying and selling the items and services you want. Funny that really was how our founding fathers envisioned a minimalist government for our country, but man cannot seem to stay away from the intoxication of power and dictatorship over others for long.

I love hard work and earning money. I have no issue buying the services I need and use. I do not think that a society that is as rich as we are should have children that go to bed hungry. So, I would put some of my lives hours towards charity, but this should be through effective charitable organizations, not the government. I believe in teaching people to work but if they choose not to, I do not want you to steal my working hours to cover their laziness. When the government wastes twenty-eight thousand a year per child to not educate children in inner-city schools, and we can do it in Catholic schools for five thousand each, something is horribly wrong. You may not agree but I think the average American knows that they and their children are becoming indentured servants to the spending of local, state, and federal governments out of control. If you keep printing money and accumulating debt on future generations and the government has the guns to enforce their will, how can you not think of yourselves as servants of the government?

Chapter 13
Health

I tend to blend health, fitness, and wellness into one category. I could split them into separate topics, but I do not think even I can pontificate enough to fill three full chapters. To me, health is something you are blessed with and cannot work too hard to maintain. Fitness is the sweat equity you put in for sports and other activities you participate in, while wellness is the whole being approach to a healthy lifestyle.

If there is any area where you are so dependent on your DNA, your health is one of them. You are going to have tendencies towards all types of diseases like my family was to multiple sclerosis and several types of cancer. You cannot change the DNA you are born with, but you can do a lot about your health. You can determine your diet, exercise level, and whether you do destructive activities such as smoking, drinking, or taking drugs. I grew up in a family with some serious health issues like my father and sister's MS and my mother's eye disease. Because of this, I believed I owed it to myself to work hard at maintaining my health and fitness. Everyone in my family except my youngest brother smoked and many of the extended family smoked and drank in excess, not exactly healthy lifestyles. You are at least lowering the quality of your life and probably shorting your life with unhealthy habits.

The concept of owing myself and god to take care of the body I was given came slowly as I matured. As a kid, I was so active burning calories in play that the doctors made my parents give me supplements. I was always at the low end of the normal childhood weight curve. Youth sports, bike riding, and pickup games such as street hockey dominated my free time so I did not have a fitness issue. As I aged into adulthood, I realized what a gift being healthy was, and I started to really formalize a fitness routine that at times may have gotten somewhere near-obsessive.

Let me back up a bit and tell you I smoked for a couple years when I was in high school and college. I came from a family of smokers and my older sisters taught me to smoke. Yes, they had to teach me since it is a totally unnatural thing to do and takes practice to get past initial nausea. Why would anyone help teach you how to take poison into your lungs? But one day in college I looked at the pack of cigarettes and said never again, I quit that moment and never touched another cigarette. Now I have heard how hard it is to quit an addiction, but it really comes down to choosing. You either want that cigarette more than you want to do without it. Or you want to drink more than you want to be sober, it is a choice. I have chosen to avoid the most destructive behaviors for a healthier lifestyle. My choices have been more towards the fitness extreme and less inclined to a diet regime. In fact, some would say I tended more towards junk foods, but I have had the exact same waistline my entire adult life.

I have a very diverse array of fitness activities I have used to stay in shape, from competitive powerlifting to running marathons. Try coaching three girls' soccer teams and keeping up your own lifting and running routines and you will find you can eat almost anything and lots of it! There were weeks when I ran six soccer practices, lifted weights a couple times, snuck in a couple five-mile runs, and played in basketball and soccer games of my own. Of course, it takes some luck to not get injured, but everyone can do things to improve and contribute to a healthy lifestyle. I had a very good friend that would always tease me about why I was wasting all my heartbeats running. I told him I was just working on assuring him I would get more heartbeats because of my running.

You may pick a different path to your health and wellness like whole and organic foods combined with yoga or dance. I have chosen a lifestyle of pretty extreme activity and avoidance of destructive activities such as smoking, drinking, or obsessive eating. Either way, respect yourself and your body and do all you can to take care of it. As cliché as it is you only get one body and even if you have a predisposition to certain diseases because of your DNA, stay fit so you can enjoy each day and have the strength and stamina for life's challenges.

With me often taking it to the extreme I have been mainly injury-free. I have had three ankle operations and a tendon replacement operation in my hand. Lots of sprained ankles have led to bone spurs and arthritis but I have been able to keep up with sports and running at a high level well into my sixties. Bumps, bruises, strains, and sore muscles come with the sports and workouts but have always seemed worth it since I always go back for more.

I think it is so much easier for you to track your activity level with all the new gadgets such as Garmin and Apple fitness watches. I think I was the last one in my family to get a watch with a step counter. Once we were all on one, we started pushing up our steps and challenging each other, for us, a day under twelve thousand steps is a slack day. You can easily get your own group going and push up your steps through a personal challenge. My extreme sports days may be behind me, but I will keep trying to stay fit and healthy because I owe it to myself and it improves the quality of daily life.

My wife started running when we were in college, and I believe even with my marathons she has logged more total miles than I have. Both our girls were sports nuts and have continued with serious fitness programs as adults. They have run marathons and done triathlons and worked out faithfully. My younger daughter has taken it to another level with a selective healthy diet. I am not sure what exact DNA mixture we gave them, but with their healthy habits, I believe it gives them their best chance for long healthy life.

Author's Intermission

By now you have a little background on me and where I came from. I have discussed how I believe I am pretty much an average American. We all have lived different lives with different backgrounds but that is why when you put us all together it averages us out. I started out in a small town and moved to a giant inner-city, worked myself through school, and I have had a solid work career. I am especially common for a baby boomer whose parents saw the depression and WWII and wanted to make sure we had a better life. Having a great wife and two beautiful daughters keeps me right there in the middle of the bell curve for the average American family.

You may be thinking how different your life's experience has been from mine, but that is the point. If you throw out the extremist on each end of the bell curve and throw the rest of us in a Waring blender, you get the American average. For generations, people immigrated here to become Americans for the freedom and opportunity the American way of life afforded. We are still the majority by far even if we are too busy with work, our children's activities, church, and making ends meet, to pay attention to our erosion of freedoms. So, we let the small minority of troublemakers on each end of the spectrum get all the attention. We may have to wake up and make time to counter these extremists, especially at the ballot box.

I have set the stage with my background information so we can move into chapter after chapter of my ruminations and pontifications. Again, I am not going to be politically correct. I am just going to try to talk from the heart. I am not perfect nor always correct, but dialogue, discussion, and debate are great ways to learn if you decide you're open to listening.

Chapter 14
Religion

With the below definitions you can see why I clearly want to separate my discussions of God from discussions of religion. I think discussions of politics overlap religious discussions closer than discussions on the existence of God. You know that the fastest way to ruin a party is to talk about politics or religion.

'Religion is a social-cultural system of designated behaviors and practices, morals, worldviews, texts, sanctified places, prophecies, ethics, or organizations, that relates humanity to supernatural, transcendental, or spiritual elements. However, there is no scholarly consensus over what precisely constitutes a religion' (Religion, n.d.). Or from the dictionary, religion is: 'A set of beliefs concerning the cause, nature, and purpose of the universe, especially when considered as the creation of a superhuman agency or agencies, usually involving devotional and ritual observances, and often containing a moral code governing the conduct of human affairs'.

Having been born and raised a Catholic in a family of devout Catholics for many generations I never even considered other religions. I attended three Catholic grade schools, an all-boys Catholic high school, and two Catholic colleges. Graduate school was my first time in a non-religious learning institution. Going to school when I did and in Catholic institutions, I missed out on today's liberal indoctrinations so prevalent in education. However, I did find myself very curious about other religions, and I selected three elective classes in college on the study of other religions. I also took several classes in Western and ancient history and found how often religion was deeply entwined with wars and human cruelty.

The major religious groups are Christians, Muslims, Hindus, Buddhists, and Judaism.

There are also many smaller, unaffiliated, and folk religions. Several of our current major religions date back centuries before Christianity, with the Muslim religion being the newest of the major religions. Ask yourself, how much you really know about any of the major or minor religions of the world other than your own. Most religions have shared principles that are very closely aligned to the Ten Commandments. You can find additional spiritual guidance such as: 'Speak the Truth' from Confucius; 'Heaven is Within' from Sikhism; 'Be Slow to Anger' from Buddha; and 'Follow the Spirit of the Scriptures, Not the Words' from Hinduism.

On a personal level, I feel the most important aspect of any religion should be to teach a moral foundation by which a person should live their life. I cannot understand how any religion can actually teach violence against fellow man. Many forms of governments over history have been anti-religions because it is a threat to set themselves up as the supreme leader.

87

Over eighty percent of all people ascribe to faith with about one-third of those being Christian.

If everyone followed the golden rule, 'blessed are the peacemakers'; we sure would have less strife in this world. Too many people claim a religious affiliation but do not live their faith. We have politicians that proclaim their Catholic faith publicly while they openly support abortion.

Sorry but in my opinion not possible. They have no moral code to claim themselves as Catholic while supporting the deaths of millions of unborn babies. I bet you cannot find any support for that position in the Bible.

As I have mentioned I was raised Catholic and went to Catholic schools as well as my wife, and we sent our girls to Catholic grade school. We may not have made every mass we should have but our girls had a strong early foundation in the Catholic faith. We allowed them to choose between the available Catholic high schools or the public high school in our area and they picked the public school. There was an excellent rating for our local public school with more academic diversity, so we supported their position. Grade-wise and sports-wise the girls did great, but I wonder if they missed out on the culture of the Catholic high school.

With virtually all religions the moral directive is clear and good for society. Read the Bible, or the studies of Confucius, Hinduism, or Buddhist writings, and you see shared principles.

I have not studied the Muslim faith or the Koran, and I have been told that it is a religion of peace. However, there are extremists that have used this religion to justify violent acts.

Extremists have used religion to justify violence throughout history. Many people have also been persecuted over religion by governments that dictate a single religion.

Or by religions that try to force their beliefs on the entire population of others. Hard to find anything good in religions or governments that does not allow total religious freedom. Religion can add so much richness to an individual's life and supply a moral compass when not subverted by radicals or governments.

Chapter 15
God

Raised as a Catholic we are taught Jesus Christ as the son of God and in the Holy Spirit making up the Holy Trinity. A more general definition of God is as the Supreme Being, creator deity, and principal object of faith. God is usually conceived as being omniscient, omnipotent, omnipresent, and as having an eternal and necessary existence. Concepts of heaven, purgatory, and hell were taught to me in my grade school catechism. Even with all my catechism teachings trying to define God adequately for me is almost unimaginable. I wholly believe in God and see him daily in many ways. All I must do is look at my wife, children, and grandchildren, and I see the wonder of God.

I have a very scientific education and business background, most of my undergraduate and all my graduate classes were in the sciences. In scientists, I have observed what seems to be a complete dichotomy of either a stronger belief in God or a move to Agnostic or Atheist. I reinforced my belief every time I looked at a sample under the electron microscope or did time-lapse photography of microbial replication. How can you look at the sky and ponder the universe and not know there is a God?

We have made such advances in science and medicine, but to date, no one has been able to bring to life even a one-celled Amoeba. I really cannot believe that this universe, our world, and everything on it was a big bang, with random accidents for hundreds of millions of years. The story of God's creation of the heavens and our world in six days then a day of rest is a simple story and does not contradict evolution in any way. If you can create the universe and have always existed, then what is the length of a day for you? Simply because God set into motion evolution with the creation of our world does not disprove his existence. I personally believe God may have intervened in our world redirecting creation numerous times over the hundreds of millions of years since first creation. I know we are here as salient beings that did not, nor ever could, create life like our own. We are not, nor will we ever be 'Gods'.

One of my close friends in graduate school had a similar background, he was raised catholic and went to catholic schools. We were both in the Life Sciences Department. He studied virology, and I studied mycology as our areas of research. He went on to law school and became a very successful corporate lawyer. Somehow, he became an avowed Atheist and a very active left-liberal. I always wondered how we became so different with such a similar upbringing and background.

My mother had as one of her favorite sayings when we talked religion, she said that there 'are no Atheists on their death beds'. I doubt my mother was the first person to say that, but she was the first to say it to me. I sure have no issue with any religion, or no religion at all, as long as a person lives their life with high moral character and does no harm to anyone else.

When I was a young boy in catechism, we were taught that saying prayers could reduce your time in purgatory. There were a specific number of years attached to individual prayers. I found one super short prayer. The prayer was three words 'Jesus', 'Mary', and 'Joseph' and that prayer was supposed to reduce my time in purgatory by seven years. I must have repeated that short prayer enough times over the years to have created a credit by now. I found comfort in that simple prayer and found as an adult I would repeat 'Jesus', 'Mary', and 'Joseph' at takeoff and landings in airplanes or other times of extreme stress.

My atheist friend from graduate school loves to argue that we had no existence or knowledge of existence before our birth, and we will have none after death. Interestingly, my wife and I had just had that discussion recently while on an evening walk. We pretty much agreed that we have some doubts about an afterlife. We thought a restart or pause button on our lives would be a really nice option to an afterlife because it has been a great ride. I think I told you about my philosophy of 'it is more fun to have fun than to not have fun' so enjoy life it is the only one you have. I have no idea if there is an afterlife and there is no way to prove or disprove so in this life, but I believe in a supreme being way beyond our comprehension.

I seldom feel closer to God than when I am hunting, fishing, or hiking in the mountains. I have sat in a tree stand during deer season or in camo on the ground during turkey season and watched the sunrise and felt close to nature and God. I often find myself repeating several of my favorite prayers while sitting there in a virtual state of meditation. I love the solitude in the forest hunting or fly fishing in the mountains, no way can I believe that these are not divine creations. I know that I could not create even one blade of grass or a leaf nor could I conceive of one to be its creator.

My mother named me after Saint Thomas Aquinas, I think, hoping I would become a scholar. That may not have happened, but I feel connected with him when I am thinking about God. He wrote what is often called the five proofs or five logical arguments regarding the existence of God summarized in his book *Summa Theologica*. The five arguments are below:

1. The argument from the 'first mover'
2. The argument from causation
3. The argument from contingency
4. The argument from degree
5. The argument from final cause or ends

I am sure no theological scholar, but I did take several college religion classes and had the opportunity to study Saint Thomas Aquinas's writings and found them amazing. If you are searching for a stronger and deeper understanding of God and how he must exist I suggest you study his writings. We had such brilliant philosophers hundreds of years ago; I wonder with as shallow as we have become with today's time-wasting on polluted social media and computer games if we will ever produce scholars of his caliber again.

We have a ton of political crap going on trying to divide us and pit us against each other. These anarchist and Marxist groups wrap themselves around slogans such as 'Black Lives Matter' and you dare not acknowledge that yes, they do as do all lives. I believe that God values every single life equally even the life of the unborn babies being slaughtered every day. God gives you one chance at life here on earth and you can lead it in his grace or choose your own path in evil.

Chapter 16
Science

Since I have alluded to my science background several times already, it is natural for me to want to cover one of my personal pet peeves, junk science. I took a total of thirty-five science and math courses in college and graduate school. I love the purity of math and biology over softer studies such as psychology and sociology. These areas and other areas of studies have been taken over by liberal activists with a far-left activists' agenda. Junk science for me covers bad science, selective science, sensationalized science, and sometimes just plain lies. I have daydreamed many times of writing an entire book on junk science or fake science.

I preferred science and math classes in college because more often than not there was only one correct answer. If I wrote a great essay for a philosophy class, I might get a C because the teacher did not get the slant he wanted from my paper. When I took a test in calculus or biology, I knew when I walked out of the room if I had an A. When I went to college back in the 1970s, I did not have to worry as much about the political views of the professor, sadly that is no longer the case today.

In good science, there are scientific methods that you need to follow. We also learn when studying the sciences to understand the difference between basic scientific terms such as hypothesis, model, theory, and law. These words have very precise meanings in science. Think of a hypothesis as an educated guess that can be supported or disputed by experimentation, it can be disproven but not proven to be true. Models are constructed by scientists to help explain or project information on complex concepts. Models should contain all the known data available and use predictive algorithms but can be flawed in the way they are built and be missing unknown variables. A scientific theory is often built on a group of hypotheses supported with repeated testing. A theory is valid as long as there is no evidence to dispute but should be challenged with continued testing. A scientific law has a large body of evidence and no exceptions have been found to dispute the law. It is a long way from hypothesis to law in the scientific world but not so often in the newspapers.

Whenever I read that the government and scientists agree to some consensus in the same article, I guarantee I must dig in and do my own research for the truth. That may sound cynical but let us put this into perspective. When I was in graduate school, the newspapers and magazines were screaming about the coming ice age. That eventually transitioned to global warming and now simply climate change. Finally, with climate change, they have given it a name that you cannot dispute since the earth has been actively going through climate changes for hundreds of millions of years. I know I just touched on climate change, which is virtually a religion to activists, so it is not open to discussion or needing further research for the converted. So instead, let us talk about DDT and the book *Silent Spring.*

Rachel Carson's *Silent Spring* is credited with launching the modern environmental extremism movement. Her book often substituted sensationalism for fact and hypothesis for genuine knowledge. Carson did not provide a balanced perspective and ignored data that contradicted her narrative. She vilified DDT and other pest control products and never recognized their benefits, especially in disease control. She claimed bird populations were being decimated while actual data showed populations were increasing. She blamed cancer rates, especially lung cancer, which were exaggerated in her book without statistical adjustments for age or tobacco. Rachael Carson and many other apocalyptic scientists and pseudo-scientist would have you believe humans are cancer on this earth. You might also like to look at the book *Merchants of Despair* by Robert Zubrin, it is an interesting read looking into radical environmentalism and pseudo-science. Robert's book refutes tirades against pesticides, nuclear power, overpopulation, global warming, and many other topics. Or investigate *Apocalypse Never* by Michael Schellenberger who uses science to refute environmental extremists. Since they have written so effectively on these topics, I may be able to skip my book on junk science.

I know I may have stepped on some toes or hurt some feelings talking about their religion of global warming. I told you I do not care about being politically correct, but I do believe in good science. I have owned farms and hunting properties, and I do everything possible to take of my properties, I love nature as much or more than anyone. Three times I have bought properties and spent years cleaning them up, removing all trash along roads and fence rows, and improving the habitat and soils. God only gave us one world, and I want to leave it as nice as or nicer than when I got here.

Chapter 17
Parenting

From many different articles, I have read the top three reasons couples fight are sex, money, and parenting. I think for now it is safer to start with parenting. I found early parenting easy because I left it totally up to my wife. I mean she was a woman and a nurse, so she had to know more about it than me! Parenting is the process of promoting and supporting the physical, emotional, social, and intellectual development of our children. For us all, it is a learning as you go process, maybe even more so for me. I am sure I read some books on early childhood development, but I am not sure how much sunk in or if any of it worked for me. I naturally believed I would just mirror how my parents raised me. But times change and their techniques especially on discipline changed, so I had to make a lot of adaptations on the fly.

How my wife took the lead on everything early on was amazing. I was not afraid of a dirty diaper or rocking a crying baby back to sleep in the middle of the night. I found those as just sharing simple chores. With my wife being a nurse, I may have whined a few thousand times 'what is wrong, why is the baby crying'. Even though she did not have all the answers, she always had patience. All the early work and decisions such as doctors and childcare were solely the work of my wife. My job required extensive travel so often I was not there to help. How my wife could get both girls up and dressed, fed, then off to childcare and on to work then repeating in reverse every day was amazing.

Probably the area that we differed the most in parenting techniques, and that caused the most conflict, was around how to discipline. I was raised by a WWII veteran and a generation that still believed in corporal punishment. If I had been out of line, I could expect a quick smack on the butt, or if very serious, my dad had a belt. Eventually, my dad could just look at me in a certain way, and I settled down. He was not cruel he just believed in good behavior backed up by a reward and punishment system. I would have had no problem with a quick smack on the butt when the girls were out of line but that was not an option with my wife. The era of public acts of discipline like a smack on the butt could bring a social worker to your home from someone complaining you were abusing your children. There is no doubt that parenting is evolving as cultural norms and traditions are changing.

There are several recognized parenting styles from authoritative to permissive or from authoritarian to uninvolved. I would say I vacillated between wanting to be authoritarian when convenient but mainly uninvolved when my wife was taking the lead. Leading child psychologists consider authoritative parenting as the best combination of support and limited use of punishments for a balanced approach. Once my wife had taken any corporal punishment off the table and inserted punishments like time out, we seemed to find that best balance as to our parenting style.

Lots of reading, games, and puzzles were the main activities when the girls were young. This led to our daughters becoming voracious readers. We still have boxes and boxes of children's books in storage waiting for the grandchildren to grow into each age level of books so we can hand them down. We enrolled our daughters in a Montessori school where they really excelled. Our youngest daughter's reading was so far advanced that when she got to kindergarten, they were concerned with ways to challenge her so one activity was she would read books to her classmates. Early on we wanted to establish a healthy attitude for education and personal responsibility in our daughters and the Montessori school really fit well with both girls.

I think my contribution to parenting really began with my wife signing me up to coach my younger daughter's soccer team. Nothing was more significant or influential in my personal development as a parent than coaching my daughters in soccer and basketball. If you add all the soccer, basketball, volleyball, and other youth activities together we had a lot of what we called 'forced family fun days' together. I think that even though the girls and the teams they were on were very successful we never lost focus that these were fun activities not life or death situations. Sports can teach a lot of key lessons which should not include a win at any cost. You learn responsibility, team concepts, good sportsmanship along with the skills involved with each sport.

If you do a great job parenting, sadly, you will still lose your level of influence as they go through high school and especially in college. You hope and pray you have given the moral foundation to make good decisions and they avoid the wrong type of people and influences. We still tried to maintain the authoritative position with enforced limitations while they grew up, but the wrong friends can really cause issues. No matter how good a job you have done every teenager hits a time when they know more than their parents, but if you can wait it out they often wake up one day and say something like boy, Mom and Dad were right! In college and beyond you hope the parenting relationship transitions into an influencer and resource of experience that they might want to access.

Here are a few pointers on how to be the best parents you can be. Remember to have fun and play with your children. Those minutes spent playing and laughing with your children are special and more limited than you can believe. Loving parents in a loving marriage are more effective parents. Loving parents are more patient and more attentive to their children's needs. A poor or broken marriage tends to struggle more when it comes to dealing with their children.

Remember your job is to encourage your children to do things for themselves. Your job is to teach them to think independently, solve their own problems, and trust in their own abilities.

We are preparing them for their role in society after they leave the nest. That is a really great job of parenting.

Chapter 18
Money

Let us continue with the areas that cause most marriage problems with the topic of money. I have vivid memories of my mother and father sitting down on Friday nights and going through the bills deciding which ones and how much to pay on each. We in no way had an abundance of money when I was a child. Dad was working his way up in a furniture manufacturing plant and Mom taught at a small catholic school for a meager salary, so money was not plentiful. With five children meeting ends financially was a constant challenge in their early years but we never seemed to want for any necessities. My mom would set up a Christmas Club bank savings account each year where she would faithfully put some money away every week for our Christmas presents. Do any of you remember Christmas Club savings accounts or the bank card coin holders? I also faithfully started a Christmas Club savings account at our local bank using the coin cards at the ripe old age of six.

Without knowing it by watching my parents I was being taught the value of money, and I knew early on in life I wanted to have my own money and not depend on money from my parents. I never thought about being rich, but I knew that I was willing to work hard to have enough money for things I wanted to buy. I wanted to be able to pay my bills and live a fairly simple life like my parents. Deep down I knew I did not want to worry about which bills I could pay at the end of a week, so I became more of a worker and saver than a spender. I was not afraid to pay for what I believed in like sharing costs at a private high school or working my way through college, but in other areas, I was very careful like my first two cars being both Chevy Vegas, the first used and the second new paid for with cash.

My wife also came from a family situation where money was tight. Her father died when she was eight and her mother went to work full time as a telephone operator. They had all the necessities but again respected and controlled expenditures. She worked as a dental assistant and had work-study programs to help with college costs and her first car was a Toyota Corolla. We were a perfect match in our careful respect of cost and value. You earned money, saved money, and spent it carefully for perceived value on things you needed. That was the simple equation we both had deeply ingrained in our psyche.

When we first married, we both had decent jobs, my wife was a nurse, and I had a job as a quality control supervisor. We had virtually no debt outside of maybe small automobile loans. We immediately created joint saving and checking accounts when we married. For us, there would not be my money and your money, only our money. From day one my wife gravitated to doing most of the week-to-week checkbook bill payments. My job was more on how, when, and if we saved and spent money. When you both come from similar backgrounds and want to live within your means, you have a lot less conflict.

Our first apartment was an apartment over a garage, and it was tiny but at only $100 per month a great deal that allowed us to put money in savings right away. The worst part about that apartment was zero insulation so our fuel oil bill in the winter was more than the rent. With two full-time incomes and frugal tastes, we were able to put money in savings for several years before we decided to have children. Starting a family was less stressful with money concerns minimized.

Most of our conflict was more when I tended to look for cheap buys when we needed something like a washer and dryer or a new car. I was often a procrastinator shopping forever for the best deals while my wife could find and buy something the same day. If I said something like we were going to need a new set of lawn furniture she had her purse and keys in her hand ready to buy.

Looking back neither of us really thought about having much more than what our parents had, a nice small clean house where we could raise our girls. But with us both working and putting money into savings and retirements accounts, we were easily able to surpass our parents' standard of living. We both advanced in our careers and although we could have spent more, we stayed frugal. When other young couples we knew would go out to dinner and clubs on weekends, we were putting that money in the bank and being a saver really pays off over time. Even in our investing, we have always been more savers than risk-takers.

I remember that when both our girls were getting married, we saw it as a chance to teach them a little about how to manage a budget. I remember hearing Dave Ramsey on the radio talking about how they gave their daughter a check for $20,000 and said that was all they would get, and it was now their responsibility to run the budget. He said it was the first and largest budget they had ever managed and that they could spend it all, add more of their own if it was not enough, or keep any they did not spend. I thought if it was good enough for Dave Ramsey, it was good enough for me. It was interesting seeing them make cost-value judgments on what they really wanted for the wedding. Both daughters came in under budget and had a little left for their bank accounts.

As years have gone by, I have never been able to shake all my frugal spending habits, believing the idea that safety and security come with money in the bank. I have seen people that drove nicer cars and had a nicer house, but often they were leveraged with excessive debt, and in severe downturns like I have seen four times in the stock market, they often had troubles. I would not have been comfortable with that kind of debt. At this point in our life, we could probably be more extravagant but one catastrophic illness can wipe out a life's savings, so I will continue to be frugal, it is part of my nature now.

Chapter 19
Sex

Sex is also one of the top three reasons couples have conflict. If you are expecting some details of my married sex life here, you are going to be very disappointed. However, I do want to try to share my insight on how and why it is such an issue for married adults. As a teenage male, there is so much testosterone coursing through your body and so little knowledge or experience that almost every girl past puberty gets a serious look. Not having been a teenage girl ever, I still guess that there are some parallel distractions for girls when the football stars walk down the hall at school. How you control these strong drives when you enter into relationships can cause conflict. Long-term relationships often expose that everyone's sexual appetites may not match exactly, which will cause conflict.

I would guess that I was a very average or normal male in that as a teenager and young adult it seemed I was horny all the time. But since opportunity and frequency are naturally limited for a young single male, being somewhat horny seemed a natural state. Once married, opportunity is not as unlimited, but all couples may not have matching desires. Couples have sexual intimacy expectations around sexual frequency with the man most often being the one seeking higher frequency. These unmet expectations often lead into communication problems and spill over to many other areas of the relationship.

I believe that there are some unrealistic expectations about our sex lives. I blame many sources from movies, magazines, and the explosion of pornography. Hard to know how much these have depersonalized and sensationalized expectations of sexuality. There is something healthy with sexual intimacy that is lost with the degrading way it is depicted in media. That does not help with struggling couples. Honest open communications and compromise along with a little imagination and planning can keep a relationship on track.

My wife has often pointed out that cuddling and a shoulder massage do not mean you want to jump into bed for sex. But building intimacy through activities like that often help you find the right level for balanced sex life. You find that there are distinct phases in a couple's relationship from the early rabbit phase, to early marriage, babies (total exhaustion time), children and teens, and empty nesters. All along the way you work together to find the time and level of intimacy that works for you. Everyone is different so do not rely on men or women's magazines for advice, talk to each other, it is simpler and more reliable.

Now, normally, I add some personal experience or a story that relates to my chapter. However, I am happily married and want to stay that way so even if I had a great story about sneaking into an all-girls dorm room for the night, I could not tell you anything about it. Or if a picnic in the woods turned a little amorous it would stay a secret. It would probably be a mistake to infer that anything could have ever taken place on vacation in a pool late at night. Almost getting caught by the children or interrupted by a crying child probably happened to other couples but I would never give specifics if it happened to us. My mom once told me that there is nothing our generation learned about sex that every generation before us did not know. She was not a prude but clearly believed your personal sex life was not for table discussions.

If you can learn to be loving and giving and if you share the little intimacies such as holding hands and cuddling on the couch, your closeness grows. When we dated, we often spent nights watching TV and my wife would fall asleep cuddled up with my arm around her. I just loved the relaxed intimacy we developed. The act of sex is not the same thing as love and can be very destructive to a relationship when a couple is not working it out together.

After covering money, parenting, and sex the three areas that can cause conflict in couples you can probably see how I ended up with an idyllic marriage without conflict. I do have gray hair and wrinkles so maybe there was an occasional stress point but no complaints here. I would do it all over again if given a chance.

Chapter 20
Politics

Hope I can keep this chapter from turning into a book of its own. I have strong feelings about our constitution, politics, political parties, and all the extremist out there. Since I believe in free speech, especially my own, and I do not believe in violence this short discussion may be the safest way to get my beliefs out. I believe I am part of the silent majority, the Americans that still love their country. The USA may not be perfect we sure beat everything else in second place.

I have already mentioned I will not worry about being politically correct. I will also not let this current cancel culture shut me up. Sadly, we have an entrenched two-party system that has evolved into servicing themselves instead of serving the people who elect them. They both want big government control or even bigger big government control. The constitution and personal freedom are inconvenient old ideas, that just get in the way of the entrenched bureaucracy and politicians controlling everything you do from cradle to grave. They have created great bureaucracies like Homeland Security and EPA that like cancer grow devouring our rights and riches in the name of the greater good. Agencies have been empowered to create rules and regulations that our representatives have not even voted on or even bothered to read and debate. The politicians have advocated the job we elected them to do, which is to makes our laws that we the public want and need, and when written, we would prefer they actually read the law before they vote on it. They arrive in Washington DC or state capitals and check their souls at the door.

One of my concerns is that if you add all the extremists together their numbers are growing. Take Antifa, black lives matter, environmental extremists, pro-abortion activists, communists, socialists, anarchists, gay and lesbian rights organizations, together with other single-issue extremists and they have all united under the Democratic party. There is dark money supporting these groups and the liberal media are complicit by their liberal slant to everything. These extremists' groups as well as most all the government unions turn out at elections for the Democratic party. And since they control many of the largest cities on each coast, they can swing the entire state's vote to the radical extreme. They start out in a national election within a razor's edge of the tipping point and if they gain a supermajority in Washington, this country as we know it may be lost.

By now you are convinced I am a Republican, but you would be wrong. I grew up in a working-class family of Democrats that were staunch John F. Kennedy supporters. Although much of that was because he was the first Catholic president. That was before the 'destroy people media'. Not sure how we would have reacted if we had any idea how amoral he and much of his family was, or where their wealth had come from. Even back then the liberal press protected its own, namely a Democrat. As a devoted Catholic family, I doubt we would have supported him knowing his personal indiscretions. But could you find me a Democrat today that would say, 'Ask not what your country can do for you but what you can do for your country'? It is more like elect me, and I will take away from others and give some of it to you.

So how do I describe myself, I am very fiscally conservative, I believe in the constitution the way it was written. I would most closely associate with the Libertarian Party, but they rarely have a viable candidate for me to vote for. I believe the founders clearly understood the danger of tyranny under kings and conquerors. They wrote a constitution with a very small federal government role. The only reasons for a federal government under the original constitution were for foreign affairs and national defense. All other key functions and rights were reserved for the states. Do you know that there were only three federal crimes under the original constitution: treason, piracy, and counterfeiting? These crimes clearly dealt with the limited role of the federal government. Today, there is no way to determine exactly how many federal crimes there are—estimates place the number between 4500 and 5000. Congress loves to create new federal crimes, as evidenced by the fact that between 2000 and 2007 it created more than 450 new crimes. Federal laws have been justified under the Necessary and Proper Clause of the Constitution, as well as the Commerce Clause. This is just another manifestation of the malignant growth of the federal government.

I had a friend tell me once that no child should go to sleep hungry in the US with our wealth, I agree but not on a government-based plan. I believe strongly we should teach everyone the skill to make a living, but they should not expect me to work for them. Remember you teach a person to fish then responsibility shifts to them. A social safety net is not supposed to be a way to make a living by not working. I believe in the charity of my choice, but not the charity at the end of a gun where a government takes my life's work from me to give to who they believe should have it as a way to buy votes.

I am often forced to hold my nose and vote for the Republican because the Democrat is a socialist masquerading as a middle-of-the-road politician. I wish we had three or four viable parties so there would have to be true negotiations and compromise. I find it impossible to understand how anyone can spend millions or tens of millions to win a seat in congress or the senate for a $174,000 job. And what are the people who are financing these politicians getting for the dollars they are spending? There must be unlimited ways for politicians to line their pockets and their family and friends' pockets if they are willing to sell their souls for the job. We need term limits to get these people out, they are supposed to serve as the citizens, not themselves.

In the early years of our country legislators at all levels were generally not full-time jobs. Local state and federal legislators were paid per diem for time served. Most legislatures were actually in session for a very limited amount of time. The people in state, local, and federal legislatures had other occupations like ranchers, farmers, bankers, and small business owners that made their livelihoods other than through being politicians. They took time out to serve the people, a widely different concept than we have evolved into today. Some states still have limited or part-time legislatures but the first state to go to full-time legislators was California in 1966. They said it was so they could have more 'professional' politicians. What a mistake, the world does not need professional politicians, I moved to California in 1980 and was in an electric service area with one of the lowest costs of electricity in the US, today it is one of the highest, thank you California for all the regulations! The speed with which a full-time professional politician ruined a state is amazing.

I have a radical idea of how to fix our local, state, and federal political system. We set up a system modeled after our citizen jurors. This would be a voluntary program with a couple qualifications. Must be a citizen with a minimum education and must complete a specific course on serving in our government system. Then you go in a random pool to be called for a local election. Four candidates would be picked to campaign for each seat. Identical money provided from tax-payer pools and limited for each candidate in each race. You can serve for only one term and your job is held open for your return just like we do for service people. After serving locally you go in a random pool for state office one term only again against four pool candidates. State candidates can go into national office under the same pool election process. Through this process, we have experienced legislators in national office, but they are never 'professional politicians' they are 'citizen politicians'. I think this system would keep people focused on serving, and with the randomness of the pool system, you would not get entrenched power-crazy politicians.

If we set aside Antifa, black lives matter, environmental extremists, pro-abortion activists, communists, socialists, anarchists, gay and lesbian rights organizations, together with other single issue extremists who have united under the Democratic party our other problem is our judicial system. The judicial system has a clear directive in that they should: interpreting laws; settle legal disputes; punishing violators of the law; protecting individual rights granted by the constitution; determining the guilt or innocence of those accused of violating the laws; and acting as a check upon the legislative and executive branches of government. It does not give them the power to make laws or to create a policy of their own. But liberal activist judges have become a mechanism of the left, when they cannot win at the ballot box, they use activists' judges to subvert the will of the people.

In the Supreme Court, we have Justices who do not respect our constitution and want to ignore the words and strict interpretation for their own enlightened policies. We even were embarrassed on a global scale when one of our most activist Supreme Court judges Ruth Bader Ginsburg told an Egyptian TV station that she would not recommend the US constitution as a model for Egypt's new government. She believes that our constitution is a 'rather old document' focused on the rights of the people, which runs against liberal democrats' desire for big unlimited government control. Beware of anybody that does not defend our constitution, they do not belong in a position of responsibility in our government. When sworn in, they all take an oath to protect and defend the constitution then ignore it. They quickly forget that they are elected to serve the people!

Chapter 21
Happiness

Really what is happiness, I would hate to think of it as only a lack of sadness or depression. Or you can only be happy if you are not overworked or stressed. Is laughter happiness? I generally believe that I am a happy person that has had a good life. But would you be happy in my shoes or me in yours? Polls say that Americans would rather be happy than rich. I believe that I would rather be rich and miserable than poor and miserable. However, I am neither rich nor miserable, so I must be happy!

Let us work on a definition of happiness as used in the context of mental or emotional states. Happiness is when we have positive pleasant emotions ranging from contentment to joy. Happiness is also used to describe life satisfaction and general well-being. I found this long list of synonyms in an online dictionary: contentment · pleasure · contentedness · satisfaction · cheerfulness · cheeriness · merriment · merriness · gaiety · joy · joyfulness · joyousness · joviality · jollity · jolliness · glee · blitheness · carefreeness · gladness · delight · good spirits · high spirits · light-heartedness · good cheer · well-being · enjoyment · felicity · exuberance · exhilaration · elation ·

ecstasy · delirium · jubilation · rapture · bliss · blissfulness · euphoria · beatitude. That is not even the complete list! If I went through the day needing to feel all these happiness synonyms, I think I would be emotionally exhausted.

I think of happiness in a much more holistic way. It is a general state of emotional wellness. An individual that gets giddy over a great golf shot then throws his club after a terrible shot probably is not a very happy person. If you think you are only happy away from work or doing your hobby on weekends that is not conducive to real happiness. When you add all the little things like a rewarding job, great family and friends, activities you like, and a relationship with God, you can live a happy life. There will be trials and tribulations and you need to work on relationships, but you can be happy and satisfied. Not happy with your job, get another job. Troubles at home, work on your relationships. Read, work out, eat healthy, live a rewarding life, and happiness will find you.

One of my daughter's friends who I coached in two youth sports was about one of the happiest girls I ever met. Whether at a practice or game she was always laughing and having fun. You could not shake that smile off her face even if you made her run extra laps for not paying attention. In the toughest competition in high school, she still had that smile or laugh barely contained even when the coach was frantic. She demonstrated she had her priorities in line and really lived life understanding how to enjoy the moment. She never forgot that sports were for fun. I hope she never loses that joy of life.

I have been told hundreds of times by my own wife or children that often I am the only one that thinks I am funny. I guess that my corny humor is not as hilarious to all as it should be. When younger, my parents said that I could knock talk out of a crack in the sidewalk. I am still not sure what that meant but I am sure I was happy even when driving them crazy with 'why' questions. At work, even in my forties, fifties, and sixties, I have been known to do a cartwheel in the office to perk up the staff. I am sure not many American VP's have done that in their office. I always found that happy relaxed staff was superior producers and fun to work with. Also please do not try cartwheels in the office unless you know how and have good health insurance.

> Happiness is like a butterfly, the more you chase it, the more it will evade you, but if you notice the other things around you, it will gently come and sit on your shoulder.
>
> **—Henry David Thoreau**

I believe Mr. Thoreau had it so very correct in that if you work on making others around you happy you will find your own happiness. I smile on my wife's face or the happy peal of my children, and now my grandchildren are such a joyous occasion. Friends and activities such as a solitary run, a pickup basketball game, or fly fishing in the mountains, it is the wholeness of life where happiness lies. Not once have I believed money is happiness, once basic human needs are met happiness lies with my attitude and actions.

Chapter 22
Morality

I believe that my parents and my early education in catholic schools really helped me develop a well-grounded moral code. These have guided my choices and behaviors throughout my life. A well-grounded moral code helps focus on what is right and wrong on a personal level and for us as Americans as a whole. If we all used God and country as a guide, we should be able to avoid major conflicts of our basic moral codes. Research has shown that people have an innate sense of morality. Even if some of our morals may vary from person to person the basic human emotions of right and wrong are universal.

When in grade school catechism we were taught the seven deadly sins. They were first enumerated in the sixth century by Pope Gregory I, and represent the sweep of immoral behavior. Also known as the cardinal sins they are vanity, jealousy, anger, laziness, greed, gluttony, and lust. Hate to say it but it reminds me of most of our politicians! I have always felt that most politicians have no moral core, if they had one, they must have to leave it at home when they head to Washington. It seems that you can find these career politicians have been for something until they are not for it, depends on who is in power and how much dishonesty they can get away with. Since the mainstream press also appears to have no moral code for honesty, how dishonest or how much you can get away with depends on your political orientation. We have had a president that was for marriage as between a man and women until he was elected then he was for same-sex marriage. Or a president and his democratic party for a border wall until they were out of power, then the wall was immoral. That shows a lack of a moral core and is only one of thousands of examples that could be detailed.

My father gave me a simple example of honesty and helped me build my moral core. As a small child, he would sometimes take us out to the factory on Saturday mornings to run around while he caught up on some of his work. There would rarely be anyone else in the entire office or factory complex. Once we ran ourselves down a little, we might sit down with some pencils or pens to draw. I wanted to take some pens and pads of paper home, but he explained to me that they did not belong to me, and it would be wrong to take them from his employer. I was saying it was just a couple things, but he explained that a couple small things later lead to larger items and anything you took that was not yours was theft. My dad valued honesty above all attributes, he hated to be lied to for any reason. What a wonderful role model he made for me.

George Washington once warned that it is folly to suppose that 'morality can be maintained without religion'. Repeated studies have shown this statement to be true. Researchers found that God's Word was directly or indirectly quoted by the Founding Fathers four times more than any other source. Without God, the Bible, the Constitution, the United States would not exist in its current form, or probably not at all, America was founded on faith in a God.

Do you know that people with strong religious beliefs donate two and a half times more money to charities, volunteer more, and have children who are less involved in crime than those with no religious activities? So, there is clearly a strong connection to religion and morality. Anarchists and communists know they must attack and destroy religion to gain and keep control.

One of the most important jobs of parenting is teaching your children moral values by which you help them develop their moral compasses. The moral characteristics your children learn early in life will affect how they see the world and behave as adults. If they see you lie, swear, mistreat others they will learn and repeat. That is why Christian schools, religious instructions, and being active in your church helps reinforce your daily instructions in the right and wrong way to act. Showing your children love and demonstrating kindness, charity, honesty, respectfulness, courage, and forgiveness will help them develop their moral core. It might also help if you keep them away from politics.

I believe many in the United States are suffering from a lack of strong moral core or a set of convictions of right and wrong. Moral behaviors and actions are steadily losing their way as the TV, movies, video games, advertising, and the proliferation of pornography become commonplace. This immorality becomes the norm, and moral values such as honesty and integrity no longer play an important role in our daily lives. The cancel culture forces people to turn their heads to the rapidly declining moral society. The problem of amoral and immoral behavior needs to be recognized and faced head-on with immediate action. I believe that a large majority of average Americans feel the same way as I do but we need to stand up and scream that we are not going to take it anymore.

Chapter 23
Love

It is time to try to describe my feelings about love and how it plays so critically in a fulfilling life. The English language has only one word for love while other languages often have several words describing types of love. We often say love when we should be saying, I like, or I have a fondness for, or affection for, or an infatuation with. But when it comes to the word 'love' itself, this one word can express all these concepts and more.

How do you feel about following sentences using love?

- I love my wife.
- I love my mother and father.
- I love my friend.
- I love a good workout.
- I love weekends.
- I love a cold beer.
- I love a good cup of steaming hot coffee.

The first three sentences use love the way they should be while the last four would work just as well with 'like'. Many languages have multiple words for 'love' having various shades and intensities of meaning. We have only one word for love in English which I feel should be reserved to express love as a sincere desire for the well-being of the one loved.

Using my limited superficial studies into psychology and my personal life experience I have tried to classify love into five categories: passionate love, affectionate love, parental love, enduring love, and love of fellow man.

Passionate love is the type of love you see in newlyweds early in the marriage and is often mixed up with lust and sexual desires. Passionate love involves intense feelings and sexual attraction for another. To me, this type of love tends to be more common at the outset of a relationship. Passionate love is part of the process of two people learning about each other and growing together.

Affectionate love involves feelings of mutual respect, trust, and affection. Affectionate love is most often reserved for close friends and extended family members where you have close and constant interactions.

Parental love is nurturing your child physically, and nurturing them emotionally. Always treating your children so they feel safe while giving them your time demonstrates your love. I also feel parental love as that deep love you feel for your parents and grandparents as well as for your grandchildren.

I see enduring love as what is built over long periods between couples in deep and lasting relationships, built strong by difficulties shared together.

The love of fellow man is part of the deep religious and moral code that you behave towards others and love them as yourself.

People use the word love and its opposite hate freely and incorrectly. You may like or dislike peas, but you do not love or hate them (well maybe hate peas is correct). Love goes beyond words to the actions beyond the word. When you get up in the middle of the night for a crying baby so your wife can sleep, or when you pick up flowers for no reason, that is a manifestation of your love. When you cook and clean up after dinner without being asked, that shows love. You may have preferred different weekend activity, but you go along with the rest of the family and make sure they have fun, which shows love. If you go along grudging and make sure everyone knows it, sorry that is not very loving. When a mother scoops up a crying three-year-old and makes their scraped knee all better with a hug, kiss, and a band-aid, you see maternal love. Working at a homeless shelter or helping a neighbor with a difficult task without being asked is the love of a fellow man. Yes, it is in the actions and the deeds that show love not the word.

My wife and I dated six years, and we will be married forty-two this fall. I think we have entered the arena of enduring love. We have been amazingly blessed but not without some sadness. Our parents are all deceased with neither father ever knowing their grandchildren. We have worked very hard in our careers often missing some of the time we might have spent with our children or each other. We have built financial security but never fell in love with material possessions. I learned that for me enduring love is about listening to each other, and it is about having a lot of respect for each other while being close friends. We enjoy each other's company but knowing how to still give enough space for each other to be individuals. We have shared almost forty-eight years together, and it is so very full of love.

Chapter 24
Evil

The war between good and evil, between heaven and hell, and God and the devil are real. I am not sure I understood evil or have to face it like my father's generation had to when fighting the likes of Hitler. I went to school when they still taught a more honest history, and we learned about the horrible crimes of mankind on its fellow citizens over the ages. Man's inhumanity to man and the need to conquer and dominate others is evil incarnate. In my generation, even the concepts of socialism and communism or dictatorships left you with a visceral feeling of evil. The only way for current generations to understand the evil of previous regimes is to study history, but that is being expunged by an altered historical indoctrination in our schools.

Evil could be defined as the opposite or absence of good. Religiously it is the manifestation of wickedness. Evil can take the form of personal moral evil in actions against fellow man. We often think of evil in the form of the demonic or supernatural because of movies and TV, but evil is more destructive when it lurks in the hearts of man. Evil is wickedness, it is an attempt to cause harm, to deceive, to dominate, and to destroy others. Evil is about a lack of morality and an attitude of malice.

I have used the word evil when referring to individuals more in the last couple of years than in my first sixty years combined. I did not understand how evil when unchecked grows exponentially, but you see it in the streets almost daily in the United States. Extremists on both ends and especially the far-left radicals that are being led by anti-American groups including Marxists, Anarchists, and revolutionaries want to bring our country down, but collectively they would have no idea on how to make it better. I consider these groups as part of the growth of evil in our daily life.

Here are some of the worst of the worst organizations fomenting hate:

The Workers World Party is a hard-core Marxist-Leninist group that was founded in 1959 by a group led by Sam Marcy of the Socialist Workers Party. It has supported the Weather Underground Organization and has a presence in the Black Lives Matter movement.

Indivisible is a national anti-Trump movement that often targets members of Congress. It is a collection of leftist activist groups. One of its campaigns asked, "Are your members of Congress doing enough to fight white supremacy?" The group states, "President Trump is a white supremacist," a term leftist throw at anyone they target. Indivisible is a Marxist activist group dedicated to disrupting the democratic process.

Antifa is a black-clad, bandanna, and helmet-wearing group of self-described anarchists and revolutionary communists known for violence and threats. The name

129

Antifa is short for 'anti-fascists'. They have become a regular presence at protests across the US that often turn violent. Antifa is basically a terrorist group that organizes online and takes a militant approach at rallies and protests. Anything they don't like is considered fascists actually making them the most extreme of all 'fascists'.

'By Any Means Necessary', or BAMN, has been in the middle of some of the worst violence in recent months. In February 2017, BAMN helped organize the fiery riots to keep a conservative from speaking at the University of California at Berkeley. They are a radical group leading the cancel culture. They claim to be against fascism by being themselves, extreme fascist.

I just picked a couple groups that are radical hate groups that are doing evil. There are over two hundred groups being funded by Soros and far-left radicals that want to bring down America. How and why individuals are attracted to hate groups amazes me, especially with so many of them college-educated from middle-class parents. Apparently, our education system is able to indoctrinate them even where there was good parenting!

Evil is not just in the organized hate groups and their drive to destroy. Just look at the growing violence in the streets all over America. We all recognize the horrors and evil of crimes such as genocide, human trafficking, torture, rape, child prostitution, terrorism, and drug trafficking. It is also the small evils like parents who demean, disparage, abuse, and cower their children. Evil can be in the constant verbal and physical abuse of a spouse. Destroying the spirit of an individual is surely an evil action.

I have not lost hope that the good of the American people will eventually push back against the growing evil, but they will have to wake up and stiffen their spines. The excuse of most average Americans for not pushing back is they are busy with work and children's activities. This excuse for not getting involved or looking the other way will allow evil to grow as it did in Germany under Hitler. We all need to get involved in counter peaceful demonstrations for the rule of law and the constitution and get out and vote for candidates that love the American way.

Chapter 25
12 Laws

I cannot tell you exactly when my father gave me a small trinket box with the twelve scout laws carved into its lid. I know it was from his childhood and may even have been his father's. My dad was a Boy Scout leader but by the time I got out of Cub Scouts we had moved to Chicago and he was not involved with that chapter. I think the twelve scout laws were the first thing I had memorized after numbers and the alphabet and they still come instantly to mind. I have asked people often if they know them and can repeat them to me, and I think only one person has done all twelve correctly as an older adult. I have tried to teach my wife, but they never seem to stick. I have found them almost a perfect mantra to build my lifelong activities around. The twelve scout laws are: Trustworthy, Loyal, Helpful, Friendly, Courteous, Kind, Obedient, Cheerful, Thrifty, Brave, Clean, and Reverent. I think if I become senile this may be one of the few things I will not forget easily.

Without trying to take anything from the scouts I want to explain what these mean to me personally. For me 'Trustworthy' is keeping your word and being honest, I believe you earn trust through actions. 'Loyalty' for me is faithfulness for family, friends, and country. I believe in being 'helpful' to others with kind deeds without looking for something in return. The goal with 'friendly' is to behave in a pleasant kind way to everyone you interact with. 'Courteous' along with chivalrous are being lost in current times but being a polite, respectful, and considerate person should never go out of style. For a scout, 'kind' is to treat others as you would want to be treated yourself, which is the golden rule. 'Obedient' for a young scout means one should follow directions from parents and other adults of authority. As an adult obedient for me means following the laws of God. When I was married my wife left out the 'obey' in the standard vow of 'love, honor, and obey' because we were an equal union in each other's eyes, obedient should never mean subservient. 'Cheerful' means to lift people up, be happy and spread joy, remember one of my personal sayings is 'it is more fun to have fun than to not have fun'. If there is one scout law that I excel at it is 'thrifty', in fact, my family and friends kindly call me frugal instead of cheap. A thrifty individual values using money and other resources carefully and not wastefully. Being 'brave' is showing no fear in the face of difficult or dangerous situations. It can be doing the right thing in the face of pressure from others. The scout law 'clean' refers to keeping ourselves, our homes, our neighborhood, and the environment clean for yourself and others. To be 'reverent' is to show profound respect or veneration for God and your religious beliefs and respect for others.

You know the Girl Scouts have a similar Girl Scout law it goes as follows: "I will do my best, to be honest and fair, friendly and helpful, considerate and caring, courageous and strong, and responsible for what I say and do, and to respect myself and others, respect authority, use resources wisely, make the world a better place, and be a sister to every Girl Scout." Take the 10 Commandments, the 12 Scout Laws, and the Girl Scout Law and you have a very comprehensive guide on how you should conduct yourself in life.

I only have one good scout story for you that I can remember. I was a cub scout, and we were joining the boy scouts on a camping outing. We were camping in a small patch of woods on my Aunts' farm. My dad was one of the adults in charge and had caught me with a small hatchet of his and warned me to not play with it. After dark when alone I was again attracted to this forbidden object and was swinging it at a small fork in a sapling and my swing went straight through and down into my knee. Luckily, it was a small light hatchet, and a lot of the momentum was lost cutting through the fork, but it really hurt and cut through my pants and bloodied my knee. I crawled into my tent and cried myself to sleep. The next morning my dad saw my injury and asked what happened. I told him exactly what I did, and he just accepted it as a self-learned lesson and helped me clean and bandage my knee which was not seriously injured. I was disobedient, but my immediate honesty was a saving grace because my dad did not tolerate lying.

The twelve scout laws have influenced my values and ethics in my adult life. They have been a well-balanced guide to reinforce my Christian teachings. I see them as guiding principles to teaching all our young, let us make sure they are memorized right after they learn numbers and the alphabet.

Chapter 26
Racism/Prejudice

I want to take on a difficult topic, but before I do, I need to remind you I am not going to be politically correct nor will I allow the cancel culture to silence me. Racism describes prejudice, discrimination, or actions directed against other people because they are of a different race or ethnicity. Racism may also apply to political institutions if the system discriminations based on race or reinforce racial inequalities in wealth and income, education, or civil rights. All people have prejudices of many kinds that are not race-related and need to be corralled as part of daily life. Claiming someone is a racist has become a political weapon thrown at any opponent of the extreme left.

Of course, you can claim I cannot know about racism and prejudices because I was born white the great disqualifier. Worst I was born a white man a double disqualifier. However, I have lived through the civil rights movement of the 1960s and seen a lot more than the kids on the streets today. I lived in Chicago not far from where the rioters were burning and looting the city. I have lived all over the United States in big cities and small and worked side by side with people of all races and ethnicity in food-processing plants. I have walked into YMCA and onto basketball courts or soccer fields across this land and made great friends. I find almost everyone basically good. Throw out the anarchist, the Marxist the extreme radicals the race baiters that make a living promoting divisiveness, and we would have a lot less problems.

Yes, we still have problems to work out together, we are not perfect, but it makes more sense to work together towards a more perfect union, not destroy a great country for the sake of destruction. We need to look at root causes and come up with solutions one at a time together. Why are the big cities' inner core so crime-filled? Why is public education in large cities failing so horribly? How do we help train people for higher-paying jobs and keep those jobs in America? We need to change the failed policies and quit electing terrible politicians instead of wasting more money with crooked people and bloated bureaucracies.

I have prejudices I work on daily as do all people. Most are probably more of a phobia than a prejudice and I work hard to make sure they do not affect how I interact with any individual. I have an aversion to extreme obesity and work hard to make sure it does not affect the way I deal with people, but it is still there. I also try to avoid street people because I have an aversion to being unclean or unkempt, anybody in my family can tell you I am a neat and clean freak. I also cringe when I see someone totally covered in tattoos or dressed in pants hanging down near their knees but that does not mean I am prejudice or racist, but clearly, I have different tastes.

I am not sure when I first heard 'white privilege'. My great-grandparents and great-aunts came over here with nothing and sharecropped to earn money to buy farmland an acre at a time to build up a farm. I assure you they never realized they had 'white privilege'. Or my ancestors working in the factories and distilleries or who fought in the World Wars I and II would laugh at you if you said they had 'white privilege'. As far back as the 1960s the idea of 'white skin privilege' was used by racial crusaders and race hustlers who believed that white skin privilege existed in our society. They believed white Americans were racist because they enjoyed the invisible privileges that go along with their skin color. Sorry, I am not going to apologize for being white or for good parents or for working my ass off my whole life to provide for my family. You can complain that I have no idea what it is like being of a different heritage or race, but no one can walk in another man's shoes. There are amazing stories of success of people from all races and backgrounds and all of them involve hard work and dedication. In the United States, anyone can raise themselves up and succeed with hard work and determination, the excuse culture does not work with me.

There is even now a growing number of professors and writers discussing 'black privilege'. David Horowitz and John Perazzo have written a pamphlet on 'Black Skin Privilege and the American Dream' to demonstrate that the most insidious bias in our culture today is black skin privilege. It means the press ignores the epidemic of race riots targeting whites for beatings, shootings, and other violence in major American cities almost exclusively run by liberal democrats. Black skin privilege means that whites are racists simply if someone accuses them. The liberal media would have you believe that white-on-black attacks are commonplace events when in fact there are five times as many black attacks on whites. According to Horowitz and Perazzo, "In 2010, blacks committed more than 25 times the number of acts of interracial violence than whites did." I personally, when finishing college, witnessed black skin privilege in the affirmative action programs in our system of higher education. I was told I probably could not get in medical school with my grades when people of color and females were admitted with lower grades.

If you have ever spent some time on the Black Lives Matter site, you will be shocked by how it has been hijacked by extreme activists. It is an insult to me as a person with a strong moral core to see that a person that agrees on black lives matter but adds that all lives matter will be persecuted by the far left. I am sure that God would agree that all lives matter. The BLM website makes some strange statements for a site that was originally founded to end police violence against blacks. Some of their mission statements include: 'are self-reflexive and do the work required to dismantle cisgender privilege and uplift Black trans folk, especially Black trans women'; and 'we disrupt the Western-prescribed nuclear family structure'; and 'we foster a queer-affirming network'.

The most disturbing in these mission statements is to disrupt the nuclear family. With over seventy percent of black children born out of wedlock, how can you do much more damage to the nuclear black family? We need to be working to strengthen the nuclear family. Children in fatherless households are two to three times more likely to use drugs, become teen parents, be involved in crime, or fail in school.

I believe that we can be successful with hard work and determination here in America easier than anywhere else in the world. If we were so racist, how did we elect a black president? We are the most racially diverse country in the world and our interracial marriage rate is at 18%. I think our largest race issues are leadership in the big cities and the people that make a living out of racism. I wish I could throw us all in that Waring blender to have only one color, but I cannot.

Chapter 27
Dreams

What are dreams, the crazy impossible images, thoughts, or emotions passing through the mind during sleep? I am more into my daydreams about life or my future that I have while awake. They are the daily hopes and dreams of human life. The dreams at night fade immediately for me but the real daytime dreams are what matters. I think for most Americans these dreams would be surprisingly similar. There are big dreams like world peace and end world hunger but most of us are looking for closer to home dreams like happiness and good health.

I have always been a daydreamer. I love using my imagination and immersing myself into fantastical worlds. Maybe that helps explain the hundreds, possibly thousands of fantasy books I have read since childhood. For me daydreaming is often thinking about or imagining something I want to do in life. I also often daydream by replaying memories over and over in my mind. My dreams are often thinking about my goals or interests still to happen. More than once, I have dreamed of winning the lottery and what I would do with the money, I assume everyone has.

I did some research to see what some of the most common daydreams are. They include new identity, travel, being famous, winning the lottery, having superpowers, quitting your job, eating your favorite foods, or moving to your version of paradise. One study said that people spend as much as forty-seven percent of their waking time daydreaming. That seems high to me in the current climate where people spend every second available on their phones texting, twittering, surfing the web, and playing games unless we count that as daydreaming time.

I spent most of my career in outside sales and service, so my daydreaming time was windshield time. I came home so often with new life-changing ideas my wife tagged it as another 'Walter Mitty' adventure. If you do not have any idea who Walter Mitty was, he was a literary character that was a bumbling man who spent most of his time in heroic daydreams. Walter pictured himself as a surgeon, an assassin, and a British Air Force pilot. Walter Mitty was published in 1939 and was made into a movie with Danny Kaye in 1947. My wife even bought me a copy of the movie. *The Secret Life of Walter Mitty* was again produced in 2013 with Ben Stiller but give me the Danny Kaye version any day.

A few of my brilliant 'Walter Mitty' ideas included opening a fitness center, building a soccer dome, buying a golf course, syndicating a soccer newsletter, owning a bed-and-breakfast, and even operating a coffee shop used bookstore combination. We found and considered buying two different closed fitness centers in Kansas and Indiana. For full disclosure and possible later discussion, we actually bought a golf course that had gone bankrupt. Of course, every time I bought a lottery ticket, which is only if it gets crazy high, I dream of all the things I could do with my winnings.

My real dreams, not my daydreams are much simpler. I find they have really evolved with the passing years. Early I dreamed about my first car or getting out of school and landing a good job. Now my dreams focus more on wanting my wife and friends to be happy and healthy. I want enough money to take care of the necessities of life such as food, shelter, and clothing. I am not in love with or need the best and most of everything. If I won, the lottery I dream about the good deeds I would love to do with the money! I still dream we can find a way to get people to live together in peace and clean up the corrupt political systems, but those dreams look bleak right now with the extremist in the streets and the vitriol in politics.

I may be mixing up dreams and wishes and goals a little, but they are very close in my mind. You could say a wish is something you want to come true which most likely never will. A dream might not always come true, but if you put in a certain effort it has the chance to become a reality. Our dreams can be big and seem unrealistic at first glance. They do not have to be as focused or specific as goals. Dreams can look out years into your future, while some other dreams may span your lifetime. Think of your dreams as your ultimate destination, while goals are the short-term steps needed to make your dreams come true.

> You can let go of a dream, but a dream never lets go of YOU.
>
> —Joel Osteen

Chapter 28
Humor

I can barely think of anything more important during these times of political correctness and the canceled culture, and with the anarchists and Marxists out in the streets, than a sense of humor. Be careful because now humor, especially satire, is not even allowed unless they have determined it correct in their twisted realities. If we really have white privilege and systemic racism, would we have been buying pancake syrup and rice with black figurines on the label? The cancel culture is crazy, for heaven's sake give it a break, and if that offends you get some thicker skin and some training on what is important in life. You really need to lighten up and laugh more while focusing on important things such as life, liberty, peace, and freedom. If you still have time to worry about logos or mascots get another job or work at the food pantry, doing something worthwhile with your life.

Maybe the problem is not enough people embrace humor, studies have shown that a sense of humor can improve your mental and physical health. I think humor is a critical life skill but like many skills takes practice. Humor can touch many areas of your life both personal and work. Both men and women say that a sense of humor is a critical quality in a partner. Humor is said to be a key trait for leaders, and it's even been shown to improve cancer treatments. Laughing is possibly one of the best things you can do for your health. I talked about happiness earlier, and I believe it is deeply entwined with humor, I do not see how you can have one without the other.

I have always been a little crazy, for example, how many times have you seen a senior manager doing cartwheels in the corporate office. I even have a video of me doing a cartwheel in our booth at an international exposition. The marketing department put the cartwheel on the internal web for our six thousand global employees. When you have a good sense of humor, people will enjoy working with and for you. When you use humor, you appear more approachable to other people. An office where humor is common is more productive and often excels in the business community. I often used humor in the office to reduce stress or diffuse a tense situation. Humor can work in the office, and it works at home.

My wife has said that often I am the only one that thinks I am funny. I hope most of the time she is just saying that in jest. I can be a little corny, so she is often rolling her eyes as she points out how not funny I am. Humor in a relationship is a vital component but must be respectful. Sarcasm is not humor and often hurtful. The better you know someone the easier it is to hurt them with sarcasm, humor used as a weapon is off-limits in a relationship. When in doubt, self-deprecating humor is a lot safer, and it is one of my strengths. When you are short, ugly, and old you can come up with lots of self-deprecating humor.

I am not a joke teller it takes too much effort to memorize and then deliver a joke. I am more of a strange witty character. I was at the office one day and one of our interns was eating a banana, and I asked him why he wasted the peel. I told him it was edible and took a bite. He thought I was crazy, and I later saw him looking it up on the internet and found it was true. The peel is edible but not very enjoyable to eat. Not sure if he ever got into eating peels but we had a good laugh when I told him it was awful. Humor is part of my philosophy of 'it is more fun to have fun than to not have fun'.

I used humor constantly when coaching sports. What better way to keep a practice light and enjoyable for children than to be funny? We always worked hard but also laughed hard. On hot summer practice I might open a cooler full of iced water balloons for a way to cool off, they loved to hit the coach with a cold-water balloon. One time before a championship game with our nemesis my under thirteen girls' team was nervous and just not focused on their warm-up. I asked if they could do cartwheels, and of course, all of them said yes so, I lined them up and said I could do more than they could, and we did them all the way across the field. They were laughing so hard they forgot about being nervous and went out and won the game with ease. They even have data that humor can improve your athletic endeavors.

In my professional life, I have written a lot of technical papers and have even published several in industry journals, but there was no humor involved. However, I took one stab at satirical humor in our college publication. The editor had an idea for a complete spoof publication on April first. We worked out a topic he wanted me to complete for the special edition. I am going to give you the complete text from that feature article in the 1 April 1974 edition of *The Marian Phoenix*.

Fahey Named 'Student of the Year'
Unanimous Decision Rendered by Judges
By Tom Fahey

Last week, by the unanimous decision of the judges, I was picked as the Marian College Student of the Year.

Because of this award, I have been asked to write an acceptance speech. This speech is to explain the reasons why I received the award and to further introduce myself since I am a transfer student.

My award was given to me as much for my achievements previous to transferring to Marian as for my numerous great achievements while at Marian.

It is rare for Marian to receive a student and athlete of my caliber as a transfer student. I felt that I should share my abilities with more than one institution of higher learning so I transferred to Marian. Until I received this award I felt that Marian didn't realize how lucky they were.

Being a playboy and lover has not interfered with my intellectual endeavors in the area of Biology, especially concerning my research on sexual habits of higher mammals. I have published two books on my research: 'Sex Made Easy For Beginners' and 'Sex Made Easy For

Retired People'. These are just a small sample of my intellectual inquiries previous to coming to Marian. My lettering in five sports before coming to Marian may also have influenced the judges.

Basketball, football, baseball, any kind of ball, you name it I am great at it. This may come as a shock but I hide my talent well. I don't want to get too overconfident.

Although I am by far the best-looking man on campus, I do not feel this fact influenced the judges' decision. I think they picked me strictly on my perfect personality and on my intellectual and athletic excellence.

I will admit that I am not the best at everything, I am just better at more things than most people are at any one thing.

Some people may look at my GPA here and think that I am not the best student, but when you are much smarter than your teachers your boredom can hurt your grades. I have yet to have a teacher that can compare with myself in brainpower.

I have continued my writing and research and am soon to release my next book which I am calling 'Sex Habits of the Bigamist'. I hope my friends here make it another million-seller.

As the number 1 student on campus, I have been asked to give a few pointers on how to become number 1. Since I will be here another year and no one could possibly rival me for my crown in one year of striving I will hold off on my pointers until next year when I win again. My words of wisdom would probably fall on deaf ears anyway.

Just because I am the greatest student on campus does not mean I will be treating the common students badly. I will continue to treat everyone equally inferior.

Again, I want to thank Joe Rea and myself for the correct unanimous decision of myself as the Marian College Student of the Year. Until my next acceptance speech, Goodbye.

I think you might be able to understand why I picked staying with Biology for my major after that attempt at satirical humor! But I still believe in having fun and trying to bring some humor to each day.

Chapter 29
Freedom

As an American, I value my freedom, but it is being chipped away at daily by our government. I realize that with a global population today of 7.8 billion that we must have restraints on total freedom of action. I often as a child dreamed of being a lone mountain man or being free like Tarzan in the jungles of Edgar Rice Burroughs. I envisioned myself in the mountains with my horse and supplies living off the land year round only visiting civilization once or twice a year to trade furs for supplies. I might have been able to live free like these characters two hundred years ago but today I would be breaking hunting laws. I would be trespassing on someone, and I sure would not have paid any income taxes. Freedom is sure not what it was hundreds of years ago.

The Constitution of the United States organizes the federal government, and the Constitution protects important freedoms. We have had a recent president that said that the problem with the constitution was it enumerated the negative rights of the government or its limitations as opposed to the rights of the government. The government was meant to have no rights but those 'we the people' granted. The government is of and by the people, our recent president apparently missed that part in law school, or simply did not like that part once he got into government.

At the encouragement of the antifederalists, the framers of the Constitution included Ten Amendments to the Constitution, known as the Bill of Rights. Antifederalists demanded the Bill of Rights as a condition to ratifying the Constitution. They insisted that the Constitution include explicit protections for important personal freedoms. Thomas Jefferson said the Bill of Rights is what the people are entitled to against every government on earth. The Bill of Rights is the first ten amendments added to the Constitution specifically guaranteeing personal freedoms and rights. It puts clear limitations on the government's power in judicial and other proceedings and declares that all powers not specifically granted to the US Congress by the Constitution are reserved for the states or the people.

Do you think of your freedom only in the big famous statements such as freedom of speech, freedom of assembly, freedom of religion, and right to bear arms? I think of freedom more often in smaller daily things like the ability to work the job I want and to live where I want or to own my home! When asked people list many rights or freedoms that we as Americans have, here are just a few: freedom from discrimination, freedom from servitude, freedom of information, freedom from search and seizure, spiritual freedom, freedom of movement, privacy as freedom. Our freedoms come from our creator and the Constitution and the Bill of Rights are to keep our government from stomping on our rights. I feel that many of these freedoms have already been squashed by our government in the name of the better good, do you really think anything is private today.

Freedom is an ideal that for many has always been worth dying for; we fought the Revolutionary War for our freedom from an oppressive English government. We have fought in two World Wars against enemies to support freedom throughout the world. We even fought our own Civil War to end slavery an abomination to freedom.

Freedom gives us the power or right to act, speak, or think as we want without hindrance or restraint from a despotic government. While economic freedom gives us the ability to earn what money we want and to spend it as we choose. We have the right to earn more than the next person if we work harder and smarter. In America, we have a capitalistic system where you can reach for the stars and earn as much as you want from your personal efforts. Repressive governments use the ideas of equality and equity to prevent individuals from owning more than another with confiscatory policies that tend to benefit the ruling class only. In communism, you will be told what job you will do, where you will live, and how much you will be paid. Socialism is an economic and political system advocating collective or governmental ownership and administration of virtually everything in your life. I can see why Patrick Henry said, "Give me liberty, or give me death!"

I consider Ronald Regan by far the best president in my lifetime and he made many great speeches but possibly his greatest was called Reagan Freedom Speech, also known as *A Time for Choosing*. The following is amazingly on spot with what we are seeing in the streets of America.

> Freedom is never more than one generation away from extinction. We didn't pass it to our children in the bloodstream. It must be fought for, protected and handed on for them to do the same, or one day we will spend our sunset years telling our children and our children's children what it was once like in the United States where men were free.

> —By Ronald Regan

Second Intermission

Well, I have been stuck in chapters dealing with sociology, physiology, and even the metaphysical so it is time for something a little lighter before we change tracks again. If you have lived long enough you can probably look back on some stupid things you have done that could have injured you seriously or even killed you. I have way too many stupid moments to list them all but a couple of the dumbest involve trees, ladders, and chainsaws. Combining two of the five most dangerous tools, chainsaws and ladders, is an obvious opportunity for disaster.

One of the houses we lived in Indiana had wooded acreage, and we had a high-efficiency wood stove in the basement with a backup electric furnace. A large oak had died and fallen partway catching up in another large tree at about a fifty-five-degree angle. I had the bright idea to shimmy up the tree trunk with my chainsaw and cut the limb that kept the tree from dropping. I mean it was not that high and with the heavy canopy how far would it drop. As soon my cut weakened the limb it gave way with the trunk starting to roll, I had to turn, run and jump to avoid the tree rolling over on me, stupid! But did I learn a lesson, nay, nay!

Several years later while we were away from home our neighbor called and a storm had caused a tree in our yard to fall on the house. I rushed home and luckily it was only a large limb that had split and was caught up on our chimney but there was no structural damage. I of course with my trusty ladder and chainsaw decided to do the cleanup myself. I stabilized the ladder against one side of the chimney and used it to climb up into the mess and start cutting. As I did the limb came free sliding off the roof taking the ladder and almost taking me with it. My only choice was to climb over the roof and down to our porch and hang from the eves and drop to the ground. After that ridiculous stunt, you can be sure I was done with chainsaws and ladders, oh nay, nay!

The next stunt was at a small cabin we owned. A smaller tree had died and when I tried to drop the tree it hung up on the tree next to it about fifteen feet up in a small fork. It had tipped only about twenty degrees, so it was not going to drop through that fork. I got my trusty chainsaw and my extension ladder to again see if I could outsmart the tree. I set up the ladder on the side away from the fork so I could cut it and the tree would then slide down the tree away from me. Seemed like a smart plan but when I cut the fork there was enough tension on the tree it snapped back and my ladder was sprung back into midair, and I found myself grabbing for anything as my ladder went over backward. I jumped on the way down and somehow avoided injury. I think I have learned my lesson no more ladders and chainsaws, at least for now!

Now let us get back to my ruminations.

Chapter 30
Sports

I love sports, not watching them, I love participating in them. My perfect day might have been a run in the morning, coach my girls in soccer in the afternoon then dash over to the church to catch a pick-up basketball game in the evening. Follow that up with another perfect day that would include a heavy workout in the gym followed by a men's softball game. As a child, I loved to play sports because it was fun. As an adult, I have continued to play sports because it brings enjoyment. We play sports because we love to play, and we love competition. We all seek out things that we enjoy doing, and I am just plain addicted to sports and competition.

There are many reasons people love to play sports. For some people, sports become an outlet for emotional expression. People like sports because they need an escape from real-world troubles. People like sports because it provides an outlet for stress. Sports can challenge us, and it can humble us. Sports test our fortitude, our courage and teach us how to face adversity. Team sports teach you to work together as a unit for the greater good. Sports and training for sports keep us fit and emotionally healthy. This is just a small sample of good reasons to play sports.

For many of us, as we get older, we enjoy the competition but have less need to win every time we step on a field or court. Just the ability to play and enjoy sports is rewarding. We may be a little less intense since we want to be able to get out of bed the next day and go to work. We sure are not making a living in pick-up games. I can now play in a soccer league or pickup basketball game and tolerate losing better than twenty, thirty, or forty years ago, but not by that much. For many, participation and interest in playing sports decline with age. I believe this is most affected by not staying in shape and the demands of family life. Sports participation starts dropping off after high school and by the time people are out of college even a few years only about forty percent of US adults play sports. The participation levels continue to drop off so that in the over-fifty crowd, just twenty percent play sports, and I bet a lot of that is golf. This drop-off is disappointing since staying physically active is extremely important to combat many of the effects of aging.

During childhood, just about every boy and girl who participate in youth sports aspire to play some professional sport. This pursuit to be a professional seems almost ingrained into our DNA and reinforced by the glorification of our sports figures on TV and in the press. But only a tiny percentage of our children will play any sport as a professional. As much as I love to play sports, I can barely stand watching professional sports. You will not find me glued to a TV watching sports, they have ruined it for me with the obscene salaries, the spoiled prima donnas, and the political agendas. Plus watching TV is wasting time when I could get in a nice run or a game of basketball.

I have tried almost any sport when given a chance but the serious sports I have competed in include baseball, softball, weightlifting, soccer, running, and basketball. However, I also have played ice hockey, tried speed skating, bowled, volleyball, snow skied, as well as golf and bike. I love the outdoors so add hunting, fishing, and hiking. In fact, if you can figure how to make it competitive, I will probably try it. When Garmin came out with step counting watches, my entire family was comparing steps each day! I hated to even lose at step counts!

Sports can be such a positive influence in life if kept in the proper perspective. I have played pick-up basketball games at YMCA's and city parks all over the US and street soccer even in Mexico. Ninety-nine percent of the time there was no racism or politics on the court only the sense of competition, your game spoke for itself. Unfortunately, I also got to visit a couple hospitals in Indianapolis and Chicago after on-court injuries.

I believe that sport influences multiple aspects of your health including your body, mind, and spirit! Playing sports for me is almost metaphysical and rates right up with family and religion on life's scale. Sports can teach so much and demonstrates the benefits of hard work and dedication that will pay off throughout your life, even though you will probably never earn a dime in sports.

I suggest all children play sports and if they can continue for as long and as much as they can. But never force sports on your children because then it loses the aspect of fun, and why else play sports if it is no longer fun. I plan on addressing children and sports especially girls staying in sports under a chapter on coaching which not surprisingly is the next chapter.

Chapter 31
Coaching

Often some of the smallest inconsequential actions in life can lead to the most important outcomes. That happened when my wife signed me up to be the soccer coach of my youngest daughter's recreational league team. I came home from a week on the road and my wife made this announcement on my new responsibility. When I pointed out that I travel so how could I coach, she answered with news that at this age, they do practice on Saturday and then a game on Sunday, so I could make time for it. Plus, another parent that had never played soccer had agreed to be my assistant. My wife's actions led to thirteen of the most important and rewarding years of my life. It ensured I would have to spend time with my daughters that I might have missed otherwise.

I may have played soccer a little in college but coaching and playing have very little in common especially with training youth. Over the next few years, I took multiple clinics and studied coaching tapes and worked my way up through licenses to a National D coaching license. I also added youth basketball to my busy schedule. I coached two or three soccer teams with both my daughters and one basketball team with my youngest daughter. My wife went so far as to get her level one soccer license and became my assistant coach and administrator. She stepped in as the coach when I was not available and helped coach my older daughter's grade school basketball team. After my daughters were in college, I helped coach a boys' team for a couple years and a couple years later I coached a new young girls' team. I enjoyed but never had the same passion for coaching other teams when I did not have one of my daughters on the team. I was told in a couple clinics that it was hard to coach your own children but mine were pure pleasure. For over a decade our family was together on one sports field or another. We often called it 'forced family fun', and it was the best of times!

I became especially committed to coaching girls because of the amazing data on how important girls participating in sports are in their outcome as adults. Regular physical exercise is good for everybody, but sports seem to add much more to the mind, and spirit of young girls. I joined several youth associations such as the National Council of Youth Sports and found that sports had extra benefits for girls. Girls who play sports do better in school and have a higher graduation rate. Sports and exercise in general improve learning, memory, and concentration, which is an advantage in the classroom. There are statistics that girls in sports have dramatically lower rates of smoking, teenage pregnancy, and drug abuse. Girls involved in athletics feel better about themselves. They have higher confidence levels, and their self-esteem is boosted through sports, not from peer pressure or other negative influences. Playing sports builds self-confidence and reduces external stress. Girls build strong bonds with teammates who support each other both on and off the field. Once I learned all this about girls and sports, I wanted to have a strong positive influence on my daughters and all the young girls I coached. Surprisingly, the positive statistics on a boy in sports is not as dramatically positive as it is for girls.

I was lucky enough to be at a sports banquet when legendary Anson Dorrance the North Carolina women's soccer coach was the featured speaker. Part of his talk was on how different coaching women were from coaching men. He described how if at halftime he was chewing out the men's team on what they were doing wrong they would all be looking him in the face agreeing that yes, all the other guys were screwing up. They never believed they were the problem. Then he described the same halftime with the women's team and how they would all have their heads down thinking they were the ones he was upset with. They would all personalize the criticism. I sure can agree with him that coaching boys were different from coaching girls.

I found that I got my best effort out of my girl players by starting any critic with a positive then describe what they could do to be even more effective on the field for the team. I found they would go through a brick wall for you if you worked with them on the positives. With boys, they only paid attention when you told them that if they wanted more time on the field, they need to make serious changes in their play.

During my time coaching basketball and soccer, I had well over one hundred girls play for our teams. We really were very successful records-wise, but I think we were even more successful building character and always keeping it fun. We were one of the few competitive teams that promoted that our girls play other sports. There was already a push back then by paid coaches and competitive clubs that if you made their club team you should not play another sport. Young children should enjoy the full range of different sports and then decide for themselves if they want to pick one as their primary sport. My daughters played multiple varsity sports in high school then went to college on soccer scholarships. I had girls that played soccer for me that then played college volleyball, basketball, and softball, proving you did not have to play only one sport for some expensive club. By my best guess, over forty of the girls that played on one of our teams went on to play a sport in college. If a girl has great grades and works hard on their high school team and club teams, they might not play at a Division I school but the opportunities for girls to play in at least a small college are excellent.

I often heard from parents that dropped of their kids at practice that they did not know how to coach. They had no idea what they were missing out on. For early youth teams, any adult in reasonable shape can and should put in some time coaching. You do not need to have been a star or an ex-pro you just have to commit to a little study, watch tapes, visit other more experienced coaches and watch their practice as well as take the local coaching clinics. The best part is you will be getting in shape and having fun with your own children.

I can think of many great memories from coaching, but I can also say that out-of-control parents gave me several issues I had to confront. I was not a paid coach even though almost all the premier league coaches I competed against were paid coaches with large clubs. I think being an unpaid coach may have made it easier for me to address problem players and parents. I simply would not put up with any behavior or un-sportsman-like behavior on the team or on the sidelines. I have coached thousands of soccer and basketball games, and I have never been given a technical foul in basketball or been carded in soccer. If a coach does not demonstrate proper behavior, how can you expect to teach sportsmanship to your youth players?

I mentioned that I coached a couple teams after my girls had finished their college careers. We moved and there was a local fun soccer league looking for coaches. I agreed to pick up a young girls' team that one of the parents tried to coach but with no success. I really re-focused them back on fundamentals. That first game came up before I could really accomplish much, and they were still raw talent-wise, and we were beaten 10-0 in the first game out. Not discouraged we worked hard and had a lot of fun and got better each week, and by the end of the season, we were winning more than we lost. Our final game was against our opening game opponent, and we won 5-3. Really amazing progress for these young girls. Now, remember I did this for free, no club fees and no coaches fees. We got good enough that after the season some of the parents wanted their daughters to try for a competitive club and caused the team to break up. I will never understand why parents think their twelve-year daughters are going to be the next Mia Hamm, or that paying makes the coaching better.

I have a large storage box still filled with memorabilia from the teams and players I have coached. The collection includes poems, letters, picture books, and paintings from individual players I coached. There are also plaques, thank you cards, and tapes put together by thankful parents and presented to me at the end of the season team parties. I have saved samples of our newsletters as well as training books, training tapes, and the report cards I gave each player at the end of a season. When they were juniors in high school, we helped them prepare profiles to use with college recruiting; I think I still have all those profiles. I love running into some of my players now often with their own children and they still call out 'hi coach'.

Chapter 32
Travel

One area that I may have done more than most Americans is how much I have traveled in my life. When you go from local sales to regional sales to national sales then to international sales, you put on a lot of miles and see a lot of hotel rooms. I have easily slept in three thousand different hotel rooms in my sales career. As a family, we have also been travelers. We have a framed US map that we have put pins into all the places we have traveled, lived, gone to school, or owned houses, and you would be shocked at how full the map is. I have worked or traveled all fifty states, most many times. I have also been to China, Australia, New Zealand, Japan, Canada, Mexico, Brazil, Argentina, Chile, Costa Rica, Puerto Rico, the Bahamas, the Virgin Islands, Saint Martin, Israel, Italy, Switzerland, France, England, Germany, Finland, Holland, Morocco, Belgium, and the Vatican which is the smallest country in the world. If you give me a few minutes I will probably remember a couple more.

With all the traveling I did all over the world, I must be honest that I was happy every time I landed back in the US. I have nothing against any of the countries I have worked in or traveled to, I just love the USA. Traveling I met lots of great people and saw many unique and beautiful places but nothing like the US. I have often been asked about my favorite place I have traveled to. Outside of the US, I think it is a tie between Australia and New Zealand.

While in a sales territory or as a regional manager of sales I averaged about fifty thousand miles per year behind the windshield, so best guess I have a million miles on my gluteus maximus while driving around America. Once I got to national and international sales the air miles really started to rack up, and I have four airlines where I have totaled between three hundred thousand and one million accumulated air miles. As I previously stated my best guess on nights in different hotels is easily over three thousand, and I hate to even think of how many different restaurants I have eaten in. I think that really qualifies me as a road warrior even though there are people who travel more than I did.

Even though I have been to and seen many places, I really did not do 'sightseeing' much when I was working. I wanted to get there, get done, and get home. Of course, when I got home the family always wanted to eat out, which was the last thing I wanted after a week on the road. As a family, we had some opportunities to mix my work with family vacations. One business meeting I attended each year was in Daytona Beach Florida in the summer, and we brought the girls every year we could. We have some great memories from that meeting including watching a nighttime launch of the space shuttle.

As an old-time traditionalist, we really believed in the family vacation, so the business trips together did not substitute for trying to also fit in big vacations. We needed to put new pins on the map so we tried to go somewhere new whenever we could. I am not sure this list is complete but I remember family vacations in Biloxi MS, San Antonio TX, Daytona Beach FL, Hawaii, Nashville TN, Chicago Il, Phoenix AZ, San Diego CA, Las Vegas NV, Orlando FL, Portland OR, Estes Park CO, Massachusetts, Nashville IN, and a couple of these had to be repeated just for fun. With so many great places to vacation in the US, I find it hard to recommend international travel for families until they have seen and done it all here first.

Have you ever seen the movie *Planes, Trains and Automobiles* with Steve Martin and John Candy? It is a classic tale of holiday travel gone awry that hits home for me with all the crazy problems I have had while traveling over the years. I have been caught in blizzards, canceled flights sometimes days in a row, missed connections sticking me in countries I did not want to be in. I have been on two flights that lost engines and had to do emergency landings, and flights so turbulent you wondered how the plane was not damaged. I have seen and somehow avoided some terrible wrecks on the highway and been in storms that just plain scared me. I had one trip that even John Candy would not have found believable.

I landed in Minneapolis for a three-day business trip with several stops planned. A storm front was headed in, but my flight beat the bad weather, so after landing I headed to the car rental area. I found that our travel agent had booked me with an off-brand rental company with an

168

offsite location, so I called and waited for their shuttle. After thirty minutes in the rain, I called again for their shuttle, which showed up loaded after having waited a total of forty-five minutes. After a short drive off the airport, we arrived at a hotel where they had a single counter with one agent who must have been on their first day because they had no idea what they were doing. I was last in line and had to have waited another forty-five minutes to get to the counter. With the major rental car companies, I had premier service, but with this one, I had to go through all the paperwork and then do a walk around with the agent for documenting any dings or nicks on the car. Two hours after landing I finally had keys to a car.

I got on the highway, and it started raining again so I turned on the wipers and the driver-side wiper broke off. I drove leaning over to the passenger side of the car to the next exit and headed back to the rental car site. I was lucky to make it back without wrecking. Upon arriving back, I again had to get in a line for the counter. After a wait and more paperwork and another walk around, I was again on the road to my hotel in a town about two hours away, luckily I made it without another incident.

Overnight the rain front brought in a real cold snap and when I got in my rental car in the morning, I discovered it did not have a working heater. I finished my sales call and headed back to the rental car company which was on my way north to my next customer call. One more time in line and one more set of paperwork with a walk around, and I have my third car. As we transferred my bags to the new car, I had set the keys on the bumper and the attendant closed the trunk and as he did the keys fell into the trunk. I did not care I had my bags, so I took off for my next destination. When I returned two days later, the car was still parked in the same place because they could not find an extra set of keys and had finally called for a locksmith to come out and open the car. I may have had a little malicious satisfaction in their predicament. Needless to say, I told our in-house travel agent never to rent me another car from a cheap off-site rental car agency.

I wish I had time to tell you another of the dozens of other nightmare trips that I had over the years that also rose to this level of frustration, but I may save that for another book of its own.

Chapter 33
Housing

I bet you are wondering where I am going with a chapter about housing. Think of it as a writer's block fill in chapter. I wanted to look at how many places my wife and I have lived so far in our life. In the US we have always been able to move from town to town and state to state. That is one of our great constitutional freedoms. However, my parents and especially my grandparent's generations were more likely to put in early roots and stay locally their entire life. We sure did not stay rooted, we moved for jobs and for fun and because we could. I think we might even challenge the number of places a military family lives in over their career. Moving a lot may be more the norm than in the past as Americans are constantly on the move in today's society.

I think a good starting place is where we have lived since being married. Starting earlier would be pretty boring since my wife only had one family home, and I had two addresses growing up, so not too much to cover there anyway. Our first apartment was over a garage in Lawrenceburg Indiana. It was small and cute as well as cold or hot since it had no insulation or air conditioning.

We moved from there to a nice apartment complex in Indianapolis that had a pond. I may have been the first or only person to ever try to fish that pond with a fly rod.

Our first big move was to an apartment in Turlock CA, where I started my first outside sales position. This position came with a car so after only a few months we started to look for a house. We found a new one we liked but to get the money I needed to sell my almost new canary yellow sports car, a Fiat X19 with a transverse engine. It was a two-seater with less than eight thousand miles. We wrote the contract offer with the car as part of the down payment and some money or he could wait until we sold the car, he accepted the offer but told us to sell the car. That was the one and only time in my life I owned a sports car. The house did not include landscaping, so I ventured into installing my first automated sprinkler system, flowers, bushes, trees, grass, and timber edging. Turned out pretty good but I never finished the backyard before our next move.

Off to Chicago and a home in my wife's childhood neighborhood. I think we were about ten blocks from my wife's mothers' house. We kind of split the distance between our new jobs, both having about a twenty to thirty-minute commute on city streets. We bought a great old house built like a small fortress that had been taken care of by the previous owner with extreme loving care. Typical inner-city block of nice houses, all in the thirty to fifty-year-old bracket and proudly taken care of by their owners. I do not think I had to do anything to the house the entire time we lived there.

For some reason going back to Chicago was not what we had thought it would be, our high school friends had moved on, and we also had changed. So, when a chance to go back to California came along with my previous employer, we took it. Before our move back we decided to lighten our load and had a garage sale. At the garage sale, a gentleman asked me why we were selling some of our belongings, and I said we were going back to California. He was surprised since we had not put up a for-sale sign yet and he expressed interest in the house. He said he had wanted to buy it before we did but was not able to do so at the time. We worked out the details, and I may be one of the only people that has sold his house at a garage sale.

We chose Fresno California when we moved back to California because they had a master's program in nursing for my wife. We went out house hunting and looked at several new or nearly new houses. One of the houses was only a couple years old with a pool, but it was dirty and had smelly cats that had shredded the drapes. It looked terrible, but the price was right. I convinced my wife to look past the obvious, that I had looked at the walls, doors, foundation, roof and concrete, and other critical structural factors, and it was a good buy. We bought it and the first thing we did was trash all the drapes, wash the walls, and have the rugs professionally cleaned. What an amazing difference, we made a great choice and loved the house, and the pool was a real bonus.

We lasted three and a half years in Fresno a new record for us and long enough to have our two daughters. Time to move up with a promotion to sales manager for the Midwest, so we headed off to the Indianapolis area again. I found a house I loved on fifteen acres in a small town west of the Indianapolis airport and bought it without my wife getting a chance to see it, not a real smart move. It was not convenient to any childcare and an hour commute to the other side of the city for her new job. Realizing it was a mistake with two small children and me traveling we found a builder and signed a contract to build a house on the east side of Indianapolis close to her job. While the house was being built, we had to figure out when to put our house up for sale, we sure could not afford two mortgages. The double mortgage problem took care of itself when I read a personal ad in the small local paper. Someone was looking for a house on acres in my area. Yes, I answered the ad and sold the house to someone from a want ad in the paper, even easier than a garage sale!

The next move was to the corporate office in Kansas City and a more stable home and work environment. My travel dropped to around fifty percent, and we lived in a house for eight years. Loving the area and our parish we found a house on three acres that allowed us to move up while still close to my office and settled in for thirteen years long enough to get the girls into and out of high school and college. Many of those years were my coaching years, and we had room to practice in our own yard. I even had a dozer come in and improve our 'soccer fields'.

I can continue to bore you to death, but we have moved three more times including a short stint in Tennessee where we owned a golf course, and boy that is a story for a long cold winter night! All told we have had seventeen apartments and homes as well as owned a couple rental homes, two rental farms, and four cabins or recreational properties. Soon we will be moving to Colorado Springs to be close to our grandchildren and to see if I can improve my fly-fishing skills. I am willing to bet this is not the last move because I know my wife still wants to end up on a beach in Florida.

I wonder what it might have been like if we had just stayed in one place.

Chapter 34
Grand Children

If you are blessed to live long enough and have grandchildren, it opens a whole new experience like manna for the soul. Your own children often seemed a task and you wanted them out of diapers. Then you wanted them to be able to dress themselves and do some of their own tasks. You were busy with work and cooking and cleaning and school and their activities, seemed like no time for yourself. Then one day, you realize they are growing up too fast. Time is flying, and why did you not make more time for them? Why don't they have time for you? They would rather be running around with their friends and then they are gone from the house. It happened so fast and you cannot get it back, no redo. They were all yours, and they needed you for everything at first; then it seems they do not need you for anything, not even advice! That was parenting, but now it is grandparenting a whole new world.

Being a grandparent is a cool engagement. You can choose whether you want to change the diaper or hand the baby off to the parents, sure could not do that as a parent. You rarely have to be the disciplinarian; you are the cool grandparent spoiling the toddlers. If they have too much sugar while they are with you, just return them to the parents. Nothing like trying to get sugar-wired kids bathed and off to bed, but not your problem. When they are sick or teething and cannot sleep, you are at your house sound asleep. You have been there and done that so why not let your children have the full parent experience. Yep, being the grandparent is a great job if you can get it!

We love the fun of being a grandparent, but more importantly, we want to be a positive influence and a critical supporter of our grandchildren's childhood development. So how can we as grandparents maximize our positive effect on our grandchildren without stepping on the parent's toes? We want to say and do the right things to support and supplement our grandchildren's development. Here are some things we want to do to support our grandsons.

I want to make sure that they know how much we love them and support them so they know they can approach us about any issue. Never let them see that you are not united with their parents on rules but make sure they can come to you in open communication. As grandparents, we want to always express pride in our grandkid's activities and achievements. We want to support their sports or hobbies as well as their schoolwork. And even if they think they have failed at something we as grandparents want to make sure they know we are proud of them.

As grandparents, it is our job to spoil our grandkids rotten. We often give too many sweets and cannot resist buying toys especially monster trucks! Oh, we buy things they need such as clothes, shoes, some healthy snacks but toys sure light up their special smiles. We already have their piggy banks to stuff, and I bet we will stuff many a birthday card with money as they get older, there will be no questioning our love for the little ones. More importantly, as grandparents, we need to channel our generosity. Of course, we all have different means but if you can afford to set up college funds or a trust for them it is a great way to take pressure off their parents while providing for their future. Whether you are helping your own children or not you should invest in your grandchildren separately and have it shielded from the possibility it is used for other purposes.

We want to be involved grandparents, and for us, that means being available to be there and to assist when necessary. Why use a babysitter when you have grandparents that have tons of hugs to give out? Having grandparents nearby means that you have trusted childcare support at your fingertips, and today finding people you can trust with your children is getting difficult. We want our grandchildren to know they can count on us. Now that we are retired, we have the time available to spend hours playing or reading or doing puzzles together. Being a grandparent is often a less stressing time of your life with fewer demands, so it is almost like a chance to redo time you did not have for your own children. When we were the parents, we were the disciplinarian now we can be the best pals for our grandchildren. With the new time available I hope to share some of my passions such as soccer and fishing with my grandsons.

We have mostly completed the arduous task of raising our own children (the job is never ever really completed), so we are now able to enjoy the simple things in our grandchildren. We can sit back and enjoy all the things that children say and do that make them so lovable like their first steps. They came up with names for us we simply love, we are GA and PAPA. Watching their refreshing innocence, creativity, playfulness, sense of wonder and curiosity seems more intense for us as grandparents. The daily stresses that go with parenting are different for grandparents, so our role is less complicated, mainly fun and games. Did you know that another benefit of having grandparents that are very active with their grandkids and have a strong relationship is that the children are more likely to stay out of trouble and have better performance in school?

Studies have actually shown that grandparents who frequently babysit tend to live longer than those who do not. So being available to babysit does not just help parents out but is beneficial to the grandparents as well. I like that grandparents who frequently babysit tend to live longer than those who do not. Of course, we are still relatively new at this grandparent stuff. I hope we can stay healthy and active for a long time to fully participate and be the doting grandparents at graduations and weddings in the years to come.

Chapter 35
Technology

I have mixed feelings about many of our advances in technology over my lifetime. There are great advances like going to the moon, computers, and electronics, and miracle advances in medicine. But I think there are aspects of technology such as social media that are almost cancerous and remind me of George Orwell's book *1984* written over seventy years ago! There is a commercial for a new TV series called *NEXT* that asks if you would give out all your personal information and invite cameras into your house and bedroom, then states 'you already have'. How many devices do you have in your house right now connected to the internet, tracking you via GPS, or connected to a camera or satellite?

Again, I love most of the advances in technology in my lifetime. We have been on the moon, conquered the atom, developed solar power, computerized the world, and put everyone on the internet. The TV set keeps getting bigger and better and cheaper. Virtually everything with a motor or engine is more energy-efficient than even a couple years ago. But there are serious negative effects of some technological advances especially in social media and the ways it is used.

I grew up in an era when we had a phone in each home, but my great-aunt's farm still had a party line. In fact, when we bought a small cabin in the Missouri Ozarks in 1995, we had a party line at the cabin for several years before a private line was available. My first portable phone was what we called a bag phone that my company got for keeping in the car. Up until the bag phone, we had a phone credit card, and we had to find a payphone to make calls while we were on the road. I wonder how many millennials realize the large-scale broad use of the cell phone is less than thirty years old. Of course, it is no longer a cell phone it is a handheld computer with a phone application. Our life has become modernized; we are constantly online using technology based on the availability of the internet. Our television, PDA's, cell phones, laptop computers, and devices of every kind have to have a network connection, or we are lost. Communications in the shape of text messages, emails, banking, and shopping are done online and now often from our phones.

Overuse of social media and technology is now known to cause several serious issues, including poor academic performance; problems with attention span; lack of creativity; underdeveloped social and emotional skills; physical inactivity, and obesity; as well as actual addictions to these technologies. Some signs that you might be spending too much time on your computer or phone are if your family or friends complain about your constant use. You need to be aware that the internet and texting may be affecting the quality and quantity of your work.

Are your constant online activities causing you stress or anxiety, or are you having physical side effects, such as tension headaches, or eye strain? If you cannot seem to stay off your phone or other devices I suggest set them aside for an entire weekend, if it makes you anxious not constantly checking Facebook or Twitter you may need to reevaluate your use of these devices.

These are the top seven social media sites: Facebook, Instagram, Twitter, Pinterest, Snapchat, YouTube, and LinkedIn. How many of these do you have on your phone or PDA? As much as I complain about social media, I have a couple of these on my own phone, but I am rarely on them. I often hear people talk about how tech-savvy the younger people are, however, I see it much more as tech-dependent. Most of the technology being used today was envisioned and developed by the previous generations. Does the current generation have the creativity and capacity to make similar leaps in technology?

Where is technology going next? We have revitalized NASA and created the new US Space Force, and we are planning on going back to the moon and to Mars. Why is that important? The race back to space may drive dramatic developments in technologies the same way our putting the first man on the moon and bringing them back did. Did you know that this year, one-third of all information will pass through the cloud, and within five years, there will be over 50 billion smart connected devices in the world? Will that make the quality of life better or make it easier to control and manipulate you? The advances in artificial intelligence may advance science and technology, but how do you control it if you set AI loose?

We have moved from horses to steam engines to internal combustion engines. We used paper then computers and into the cloud. We quickly moved from landlines to cell phones and Bluetooth, as human beings we blindly charge forward to new technology. We have always embraced technology, sometimes grudgingly but if it makes our life better, we will eventually embrace it.

Chapter 36
Miscellaneous

This miscellaneous chapter is to catch some of my favorite topics or activities that simply do not deserve their own chapter.

Weightlifting was a major part of my sports activities for over fifteen years. When I got to grad school, the organized sports opportunities were mostly over, so I picked up weightlifting. I liked it for the simplicity of you against gravity. I did not want to get big that is for bodybuilders, I just wanted to get stronger, so I competed at the 65-kilo weight class which is about 148 ¾ lbs. While traveling in a sales territory I found all the good gyms for powerlifters in my territory. I had a lot of success in competitions and at thirty-seven I competed in the NASA nationals and won my age and weight class and won while setting a world record in the dead lift. That was special since my wife and two young daughters were there cheering me on. With my growing coaching commitment in soccer and basketball, I set aside competition after that, but I have always kept strength training part of my fitness program.

After setting aside weightlifting as a competitive sport, I needed to pick up something to fill my addiction to sports, so I decided to get serious about running. I had always jogged but did not like it other than it supported my health and other sports activities. I was still traveling so taking a pair of running shoes anywhere with me was easy. I remember I was in Las Vegas and went out for a run and got turned around, and the road did not go through so before I got turned around and back to my hotel, I had run over six miles. When I told my wife, she suggested I try to run a local half marathon with her coming up in a couple months. I must tell you I do not like to run; I have never liked to run; I only like being finished with a run! Since I was not competing in weightlifting anymore, I needed a focused challenge, so I agreed.

Well, I ran the half marathon and did pretty good and then in a moment of insanity I declared I was running the fall Kansas City Marathon in five months. I learned that running a marathon was not twice as hard as a half marathon it was more like logarithmic or ten times harder. I trained with three other people but when I lined up that fall at the start line, I was the only one left; they had all dropped during the process to training injuries. The Kansas City Marathon had a special award for the fastest first-time marathoner over forty, I came in second less than a minute behind, and that whet my appetite for even faster times! I trained even harder, and the next year, I ran three marathons in ninety days and qualified for Boston with a 3:17 at the Chicago Marathon. That result put me into the top one percent of people completing marathoners in the US. Although I have always kept running, I burned out that year and have never even thought of doing a marathon ever again.

When you are growing up and there are three family farms hunting comes naturally. I remember going out with my dad hunting for rabbits, squirrels, quails, and pheasants. When I was growing up, we did not have deer and turkey in the area around my aunt's farms but now they are lousy with them. As an adult, I have been an avid deer and turkey hunter, and now in retirement, I hope to have more time for additional hunting activities. I have found most hunters love the land and are excellent stewards of the land. We have owned several properties, and I have spent extensive time cleaning up and improving the properties I owned. At least twice a year, I would walk the road frontage of our properties and pick up trash thrown out the windows of passing cars. I always wondered how many of the people throwing trash out their windows were true outdoorsmen.

I am going to get politically incorrect here because when I was a teenager and into my twenties, I was an avid fur trapper. My uncle started trapping the areas around our farms and with permission from our neighbor's farms resulting in a large area available for us to trap. He had started trapping back in the 1950s to supplement his income. Some of my earliest memories at the farm were watching my uncle head out to run his trap line and coming back with muskrats, raccoons, and mink. I was fascinated and could not wait until I was big enough to walk the riverbank with him. He taught me well and by the time I was a teenager he assigned me my own area to trap. Eventually, I took over the trap line completely during times I was out of school for winter vacation. My uncle would drive and pick me up while I made all the sets and ran the trap line early every morning. One trapping season I made enough to pay my entire years of college tuition. The fur market collapsed with animal right activists and has never recovered but there were many a great day with my uncle on the rivers I will never forget.

I do have one favorite sedentary activity and that is reading. My wife and I together with our children have probably spent a small fortune on books. We mostly use our phone or PDA's to read now but there is nothing like the feel of a hardback book in my hands. I started to keep track of each book and author with a small note and a grade. I have been averaging reading between ninety and one hundred books a year. I often get asked what I like to read, and my answer is everything from business to science fiction. Sadly, Americans lag behind most of the world in reading books. We are too busy playing video games posting on Facebook and Twitter to read a book.

The only other activity I really like and have not commented on is fishing. Now I am not one of those fanatic bass boat-type guys. We have owned a cabin with ponds, and I was the kind of guy that liked going out for thirty minutes in the early morning and late evening and catch and release a few fish. I also love to trout fish in small high mountain streams and make regular trips to Colorado. I love to hike into areas where I will not see another person fishing which gets harder every year. There is one remote stream I hike to that is at about nine thousand feet elevation, and I have been fishing it for over twenty years. I really feel close to God when I am out alone in the mountains hiking or fishing.

I must tell you a little about the golf course we bought. It was sold to a bank at auction on the county court steps after the second bankruptcy. The bank that bought the course was the biggest debt holder. After they took over the course, they found my business card in the previous owners' desk at the clubhouse. My brother and I had fancied we would buy it a year earlier, but it was a mess and way too much money for us. The bank made me an offer I thought I could not refuse, asking only what the land was worth valued as farmland.

My wife and I went down to look it over and thought why not take a chance! We had to immediately pour sweat and money into the place since it was barely a golf course by the time, we took possession. Luckily, I kept my job for safety and the continued income while we reopened the course. After about six months of blood, sweat, and tears we hit our first summer month in the black. We immediately put the course up for sale with a broker and escaped with a quick sale at break even and were we ever thrilled to escape that venture. A golf course is eighteen holes you pour money into, and it never pays off. Over 800 hundred golf courses have closed in the last decade, and we should have let this one stay closed. The new owners lasted only one year.

Final Intermission

I was daydreaming the other day and decided to list just a few of the things I love.

- I love the joyous laughter of the toddler.
- I love the four seasons of the Midwest, springs arrival, the depth of foliage in summer, falls colors and winters stark black and white contrast.
- I love when my wife rolls her eyes at my poor attempts at humor.
- I love the anticipation of that first cast in my favorite trout pool high in the mountains.
- I love the feeling of hitting a perfect drive down a golf fairway.
- I love looking at the full moon on a crystal-clear night.
- I love lying in bed and listening to storms rumbling in with the lightning and thunder followed by the rain on the roof.
- I love dreaming about tomorrow's opening of deer season.
- I love the sparkle in my wife's eyes when I bring flowers just because.

- I love it when I am done with a good run.
- I love the smell of freshly mowed lawn.
- I love a great campfire with or without the smoke.
- I love a great wood fire in my fireplace, not a gas fireplace.
- I love to read a good book.
- I love to just sit in the woods in the morning and listen to the spring gobblers.
- I love to just take in the size and majesty of an ancient oak tree.
- I love doing puzzles with my wife watching the intensity she puts into the task.
- I love Christmas morning and the magic in the air children give it.
- I love working in a garden then sharing the harvest.
- I love a good pick-up basketball game with friends at the church gym.
- I love burning leaves and the smell of burning leaves just not the raking part.
- I love when my wife snuggles up and falls asleep under my arm on my chest.
- I love when morning breaks with me in a tree stand and if unsuccessful when the sun sets from that same stand because the hunting is its own reward.
- I love teaching a skill to the young and seeing joy in their eyes when they accomplish it.
- I love working with my hands and seeing the results of simple labor.

- I love to BBQ but, even more, eating it.
- I love the hugs from my children and now my grandchildren.
- I love simple family downtime.
- I love the open road to almost anywhere, and the back roads through tall corn and thick soybeans.
- I love to bring a smile to someone's face.
- I love rocking a crying baby back to sleep in a rocker in the middle of the night.
- I love looking at a full moon and dreaming about the heavens.
- I love the sounds and smells of the ocean.
- I love the beauty of a flower garden with butterflies and bees dancing on the blooms.
- I love the burn of a great workout in the gym.
- I love when my grandchildren crawl up into my lap.
- I love watching old movies like *Mary Poppins* and *The Wizard of OZ*.
- I really just love life!

I suggest you make your own list of things you love and take it out and read it when you are having a tough day.

Chapter 37
Aging

I find aging an interesting topic if you have lived long enough to put some perspective to it. The dictionary keeps it simple by saying aging is 'the process of growing old'. Data shows that by 2030, the number of Americans age 65 and over is projected to reach some 71.5 million people, with nearly 10 million of them 85 and older. In addition to that, many seniors today report better health, greater wealth, and higher levels of education than past generations. That sounds pretty good if you are in your fifties but if you are retired it can be looked at another way completely, we drop by some 61.5 million people in the first twenty years of retirement! Not complaining just looking at the facts!

If you do a little internet research on aging most of the information is on how to live a longer life, yeah, of course! The obvious items for a longer life are: do not smoke or drink to excess, stay active and eat a healthy diet, and stay social and positive. You will also find articles on all the negative things that will happen to you as you get older such as hardening of the arteries, diabetes, bladder, and bowel issues, the list is very long and somewhat depressing. It is a little harder to find articles detailing all the positives about aging.

But I did find some material that listed some positives about aging. We mellow with age and generally our happiness increases. Super seniors in their 70s and 80s report being less troubled by anger, stress, and worry than the younger age group. Surprisingly to me, rates of depression go down after age 60. We also maintain our wisdom and experience-based knowledge well into old age. Married seniors report greater satisfaction and more positive experience than younger married couples. Studies even show that seniors have a higher level of happiness. I think as seniors we have reached a level of self-awareness in life's realities that allows us to focus on the positives of aging over the negatives.

I read an article that breaks the life cycle of aging into twelve stages. They include conception, birth, infancy, early childhood, middle childhood, late childhood, adolescence, early adulthood, midlife, mature adulthood, late adulthood, and death. That is a little too complicated for me and heavy on childhood, so I think it works best for me to break the aging process into the decades I have lived.

My first decade (let us call it childhood) was all about both a biological and emotional dependence on my parents. You start out as a blank page to be written upon. Early childhood is the beginning of the discovery of life's wonder. Nurturing parents are your whole world. As you age you start with experimentation, everything had to be touched or go in your mouth. I learned to communicate, and they learned how to say no! Playtime leads to creativity and social interaction. Over time in this first decade, my personality and some independence developed. I really had fun and had no concept of aging beyond what number my next birthday was. Summer vacation was too short, and the school year was too long.

Now my second decade (simply my adolescence) was a rush. We moved from a small town to a megacity, and back to a small town in less than a decade. Between eleven and twenty years old crazy things happen such as puberty that brings a world of challenges. I changed physically, and felt new complex emotions, and had new social interactions. Experts will tell you being a teenager is harder than being an adult, but I must have missed that because I sailed right through this decade. The school was pretty good, as far as schooling can be for a teenager.

Getting a driver's license was great, even though I failed my first two tries with the driving instructor. Dating was a great new experience, and I had good part-time jobs to put spending money in my pocket and in the bank. Probably the toughest part was my parents' both had serious health issues which forced me to grow up faster than a lot of my friends. I lost a grandparent and all my great-aunts so for the first time I faced the reality of morality, but that was still for old people. This is a decade when if you are asked how old you are you always respond with 'I am going to be'. I was still waiting and wanting to get older!

My third decade was a tumultuous time of growth and change. I am really on my own now and my personal responsibilities increase enormously. This is my decade to finish college and graduate school, get married, buy our first home, and start building a stable career. Gone are some of the carefree days of fun and games, but not all gone! This was when I had to establish a stable life and start to make my way as an adult. I was still never really thinking about aging even though I lost my father to cancer. Yes, death became a real thing but not something to dwell or fixate on. I am still young, healthy, not peaked out athletically, and still looking forward to my next birthday. I married at twenty-five and my first daughter was born only a couple of weeks before my thirtieth, so I was free of parenting responsibilities. Overall, a really great time of my life with my wife and life's best friend.

Time to move on to the decade often called midlife, and so often connected to the famous midlife crisis. Going from thirty to forty involved heavy parenting, career advancement, and a non-stop children's activities agenda. I do not think I had a midlife crisis because each week was already in crisis management. Looking back, this decade brought two little girls to raise, plus we moved three times, and my wife and I both made major career moves. By the time you hit forty, you are realizing you will not live forever and that your body may be aging! For the first time, I was reflecting on life, my career, my relationships, and what I wanted to accomplish going forward. Aging and the end of life are still at best something you might contemplate but not worry about.

I will tell you from forty to fifty aging becomes a reality. My daughters went from eight and ten to eighteen and twenty during this era. They became teenagers and automobile drivers both terrifying to all parents. My wife and I became dumb while they came to know it all. They moved from grade school to high school and on to college in this every quickening sprint of years. I had a doctor tell me once that as humans we start a sharp physiological decline after age forty. Well, I can attest to that because my runs got shorter and slower. My weight training yielded constantly lower results. I had to get reading glasses and an ankle operation on bone spurs, and I was told I had arthritic degeneration in my ankle. Oh, yeah, the aging process was not to be denied by any amount of exercise or diet. I lost a couple friends and acquaintances to things such as cancer and heart attacks. And you first start to think about end-of-life things such as more life and long-term care insurance, as part of plans to take care of your loved ones.

I think I mellowed from fifty to sixty. We were empty nesters most of the time and our careers were topping out with some nice results so we could really build a little nest egg for retirement. Of course, there are stressful things such as daughters' marriages but in that area what can a dad do but exactly what his wife and daughters tell him to. Two more ankle operations remind me that the body is not as young as I once was, but I still have an active fitness regime to stay in shape. In fact, I have had the exact same belt size since high school, not sure many people can say that. But it takes longer to heal and after a basketball or soccer game, I hurt all over the next day. Being more mature and stable and financially secure is nice but aging sucks!

I cannot tell you the complete story of the sixties because I am still living them. I retired at sixty-five and somehow it has been crazier than when I was working full time. My wife and I still run and work out but if I told you how slow we run now you might laugh, but as my wife states, "At least we are still doing it!" I still try a little basketball and soccer but now it takes two or three days to quit hurting. You can fight aging with a fitness program, and it improves your quality of life but prepare to be sore.

Another thing that really struck me when I hit sixty was the realization that all the things, I was going to do in life probably were not going to happen. The many 'Walter Mitty' dreams were just those dreams. That is not all bad, but some dreams die hard.

Billy Graham the preacher in his nineties in an interview said that he was at peace and prepared to meet his maker but what he was not prepared for in old age was becoming so feeble. I am a long way from feeble, but I can just start to grasp what he was feeling. If we are lucky enough to live a long life we will go from dependency to independency and vice versa. Hopefully, I can update you next decade when I am in my seventies.

Chapter 38
Bucket List

The expression *Bucket List* first came into wide use following the release of the film *Bucket List*, in December 2007. Immediately after the movie and for some time after only people who feared their imminent death compiled a bucket list. Over the years it has become more widely used to be a list of things or goals that you want to do someday. I like the broader use as a wish list since it is a less morbid view for the bucket list. The reality is that no matter what your age you just never know when you are going to die. So, to keep a bucket list of things to do before your death may mean putting off what you desire most, so you should work on that wish list continuously.

We all need a list that can give our life purpose and direction. Your list can focus on learning and experience, which will create precious memories. Simple goals such as exploring and discovering new places and activities give you something to strive for in daily life. Your list is not a one-time thing but should be reviewed and renewed as you go along. We should make this our living list and start enjoying things we dream about today not at some point down the road.

If you go online, you will be amazed at how many people want to help you build your bucket list. You will find articles such as *281 Awesome Bucket List Items You Should Add to Your List* or *Bucket List Ideas: 101 Things to Do Before You Die* or even *543 Bucket List Ideas. No More Excuses.* But to me that is not how it works, you do not look at others' made-up list, you look inside yourself for what will fulfill you and make you happy. My list would be dramatically different than yours because I have traveled so much during my lifetime and seen many of the sites and countries people might put on their bucket list. I am going to share with you many of the activities that I might enjoy greatly to do or do again in this lifetime.

- Fish a back-country mountain stream rarely fished by other people
- Hunt big games such as elk, bear, moose once in my life
- Learn to relax and enjoy the holiday seasons more fully
- Grow much older with my wife
- See the rest of the great sites in the United States I have not seen yet
- Travel Alaska again more fully
- Take my wife to Australia and New Zealand
- Hit at least one hole in one which may mean a lot more golfing
- Coach my grandsons in soccer
- Visit more of the great state fairs, I have seen nine with Indiana over a dozen times

- Jog thousands of more miles with my wife
- One more business venture of some kind
- Read another thousand books
- Float some of the great rivers in a kayak
- Have a beach house for a month during the winter
- Have a mountain lodge for a month in the summer
- Spend a week at the Smithsonian
- Own a boat
- Do a thousand more puzzles with my wife
- Finish visiting the National Parks
- Track down and spend some time with high school and college friends
- Walk and trap a small stream near my Aunts farm one last season
- Help people clean up and rebuild after a natural disaster
- Write a book worth reading
- Travel to Ireland to where my ancestors lived

You might notice that my 'living list' is a lot of the things I have done that I want to keep doing. It is not a crazy list of impossible items but has several challenges that are worth pursuing.

I recommend creating your own 'living' bucket list.

Chapter 39
Naturalist

If you have been following along with me through all these reflections you may have picked up on my love of the outdoors and outdoor activities such as hiking, hunting, and fishing. I prefer outdoor sports to indoor sports. Even basketball is more fun on a good outdoor court. I love good old mother nature. Surprisingly if you look up the word nature in different dictionaries they vary and even seem to struggle with just how to define the word nature. One dictionary describes it as all the animals, plants, rocks, oceans in the world. Another source describes nature as all the features, forces, and processes that happen such as the weather, the sea, mountains, the existence of plants and animals. As humans we are all part of nature, not apart from nature.

I might best describe myself as a naturalist which is a person who studies nature and especially the plants and animals as they live in nature. Since I have degrees in Biology and Life Sciences, I think a naturalist fits me closer than calling me an environmentalist. I am definitely not a tree hugger or an environmental extremist, but I do believe we need to be good stewards of the land. Coming from a legacy of farming families and having owned land and farms myself, I have a deep understanding of the responsibility that you are a steward of the land for future generations that will be working, living off of, and enjoying that same land.

We have owned a golf course with two hundred and twenty-five acres, two farms, and four recreational properties and managed them all to improve their beauty and keep them clean and natural. We have hauled off truckloads of trash and worked with the department of natural resources to design plans to improve the properties. I regularly walked the frontage roads on our properties and picked up the trash that people threw out their car windows. We loved and respected each property always keeping it cleaned and groomed.

Some people think the problem with mother nature is man himself. The environmentalist Rachel Carson said, "Man is a part of nature, and his war against nature is inevitably a war against himself." Many of the more extreme environmentalist leaders in the movement reveal attitudes that are decidedly anti-human. I am much more practical believing we are smart enough to keep the planet healthy while continuing to build and develop infrastructure for humans. Alarmists were screaming over seventy years ago that we could not support the population explosion. Mass starvation and disease were inevitable. Of course, that was when we had several billion less people on the earth.

When I am standing near a mountain stream, hunting in the woods, riding an ATV through the fields, or sitting at a firepit at night looking at the stars I am amazed at what God gave us to enjoy. Some people struggle with believing in God, but how can you look at the stars through a telescope or a single cell under a microscope and not see god. I guarantee you that we could not create either, and it was not a random accident. There is creation versus evolution debate that tries to frame creation being religious and evolution as being scientific. However, as a scientist I find they fit perfectly. God created the heavens and earth and all the creatures and made evolution part of his grand plan. Since all the biological systems he created can evolve via changes in DNA, why is there any debate. You may believe we evolved from apes or similar, but I believe God placed us here when the world was ready for us from the millions of years it took for our planet to mature. I see divine guidance in so many places in nature, and I think that it is still occurring. Our scientists are trying to break down and reverse engineer everything, but they can only discover what God has created.

Everyone needs to turn off their phone, PDA, and other electronics and go somewhere peaceful, such as the countryside or for a walk in the woods. Rather than sitting on the sofa take time to appreciate the outdoors and things mother nature has provided. We all spend too much of our lifetime working and nowhere near enough time relaxing and enjoying nature. Slow down, work less and look at a butterfly or a rose, pick up an acorn, and dream about the potential for it to be a one hundred foot tall oak tree, God and nature are all around you, and it is so miraculous to behold.

I want to share one of the most amazing occurrences I can remember while out on our farm. We had cut trails throughout our property for hiking and ATVs. Late one afternoon I walked down across our pond damn and into a tunnel-like lane through a very thick patch of forest. As I entered this area it virtually came to life with thousands, possibly tens of thousands of Monarch butterflies. I would assume they were on their southern migration. They were everywhere and as thick as heavy snowflakes but much more colorful. Do you know that in a quiet place like where I was you can hear each flap of their relatively big, solid wings? I could not make out individual butterflies but could hear their collective wing noise. That was a once-in-a-lifetime!

Chapter 40
What-Ifs

I have asked myself hundreds maybe thousands of times 'what if'. If I tried to make a complete list of my 'what-ifs', it would seem endless. My what-if time is usually looking back on my choices and how they set my path in life. Different choices would have led to an entirely different life, or would it have? My what-ifs cause me to reflect upon the question of free will versus destiny. During our lives, we face the contradictory claims that our lives may be predetermined. Our destiny is set by God and therefore we are just playing it out. However, I believe that our lives are the results of our choices and that we shape our daily decisions as we go along. I believe we have free will and make our choices using that free will, but God already knows the choices you are going to make. That is deep thinking for me not being a philosophy or theology major, so let us lighten it up and just go over some of the 'What if's' I have pondered at different times.

One of the first big turning points in my life involves my dad taking the job in Chicago, what if he had not taken the promotion. If we had stayed in small town Rushville, would I have even gone to college? I might have gotten out of high school and went to work in a factory or on the farm. I sure would have never met my wife who is from Chicago. Absolutely nothing would have been the same from age twelve on! Or maybe I would have still gone away to college and met my wife who somehow ended up at the same school, our paths still pushed together by destiny. Who knows but interesting to contemplate?

Just look at the list of jobs I have had over my life. There have been dozens of career choices that if made differently would have led to completely different paths. What if I had never moved from an inside QC position to an outside sales job? What if we had never moved to California? Much of my adult personality was determined by needing to interact effectively with people as a salesman, prior to that I was somewhat introverted. My wife has pointed out that her choice of Fresno to study for her master's degree in nursing or when we decided to try and start a family were giant "what if's" in our lives. The reality of recombination of DNA means that if we had even changed the days of conception our children would be different, or would they be different, maybe destiny at play again!

Another area where I have pondered what if is in our housing choices. That may seem like small decisions, but they are enormous in their effect on my life's path. The first two houses may not have had what if effects on our life path since it was just my wife and I, and we were working close by, and we did not have children yet. But after that, each house choice had direct impact on ourselves and our children. One example is when we moved to Kansas City, I wanted to live on a property way out of the city, and we looked hard but, in the end, we bought in town. We bought near a great Montessori school where our daughters excelled. We were in a good parish with an outstanding private Catholic school which they attended. They joined youth sports teams, and I became a coach, much if any of this would never have happened if we had bought on forty acres out of town. They might have ended up riding horses. If they never played soccer there would have been no soccer scholarships for college. Or maybe somehow most of this would have happened no matter what house we purchased?

You make decisions every day, how many of those are 'what-if' decisions? Changing jobs and moving into a new house are obvious life-changing decisions. What schools your children go to have major effects on their life. But there are the many small things that also add up to how your life will be played out. What if tomorrow you stayed positive at work and came home and spent better quality time with your family instead of drinking a beer in front of the TV? What if this weekend you loaded up the family and headed out for a day walking trails at the state park? What if you decided to stop smoking and started walking a little each day? See each day is full of 'what-ifs' and they are unlimited opportunities. Maybe in ten years, you can say what if I had not stopped smoking, I would not be enjoying my grandchildren today!

My biggest personal 'what-ifs' from my past are numerous but here are some of the really big ones.

- What if I had not stopped smoking?
- What if I had not married my wife?

- What if I had not had children?
- What if my mom and dad had been around to know my children?
- What if my wife had not signed me up to coach youth soccer?
- What if we had not picked the neighborhood in Kansas City we did?
- What if we had had enough smarts to have not bought a golf course?
- What if I had applied to medical school and gotten in instead of going to graduate school.?
- What if I had picked different in a couple of my career changes?

All of these what-ifs are direct influencers on life's path, and having made any of these differently would have led to an entirely different life result. Of course, I often felt some outside or greater influence in major decisions so maybe I would still be sitting here writing even given some different decisions!

Chapter 41
Death

I doubt dwelling on death has much practical use beyond noting that birth and death are the bookends of our lives. But you might be surprised how much time some of the great philosophers have spent contemplating death. Plato, possibly the greatest philosopher of Antiquity was convinced that after death, souls were judged. Good souls were thus led to the islands of the blessed, and the bad souls were chastised. This is very close to Christian beliefs that spirits are eternal and, if you were a good person, your spirit will go to heaven. On the other hand, hell awaits those who have led a sinful life. Albert Einstein in his obituary stated, "I cannot imagine a God who rewards and punishes the objects of his creation… Neither can I believe that the individual survives the death of his body, although feeble souls harbor such thoughts through fear or ridiculous egotism."

I know that for me the only time I really thought about death earlier in life was when a family member or friend died. Then as you pile up the years yourself, the reality and the inevitability of your own death creep into your consciousness. It seems that death starts almost like a shadow in your peripheral vision, but the shadow grows with each succeeding year. Recognizing the inevitability of death in time gives life a direction and framework within which to understand aging and the changes of life. Even the concept of death looks very different to the young than to the old. Mortality really takes on its own reality as we age. Young adults have an intellectual understanding that death comes to us all, but it can easily be ignored for the time being. By ignoring the end-of-life issues, we can feel safer and focus only on living and daily activities.

I have no idea how many times I have heard the phrases 'the only two certainties in life are death and taxes', or 'death is the great equalizer' these are humorous ways to deal with the realities of death. As a Catholic every year we are reminded of our mortality on Ash Wednesday when reciting the phrase '*Remember man that thou art dust, and unto dust thou shall return'*. I do not plan on an obsessive rumination on death because I think a focus on life is more productive. It is effective to think about death only to the point that it drives us to live more fully in life. Eventually, all of us will die, it is part of the reality of human existence but no reason not to wish it off a far as possible into the future.

In college and graduate school, I had several friends that were psychology majors and they loved to sit around and talk about morbid topics such as death. Their consensus was that we did not exist before conception and had no awareness, and when we die, we will again cease to exist with no awareness of any kind. Their deep thinking was usually done when they were drinking and or smoking a little marijuana. They were all avowed atheists or agnostics at least while at school. But I would not be surprised if they were going to church with their parents when they were home on holiday. I would never have trusted any of them to council real people after they finished with their degrees. I always wondered how many of them would get religious when they were facing a terminal illness.

I have no special insight or knowledge of life after death. You can study many different religions and their view of death range from reincarnation to resurrection. Age seems to bring people more to the conventional belief in life after death, a survey of people 50 years and older found that seventy-three percent believe in an afterlife. With women even more likely to believe in an afterlife by eighty percent to men at sixty-four percent. In this same survey, sixty-seven percent of the people confided that their belief in a life after death has increased as they have gotten older.

Remember I am born and raised as a Catholic so Jesus, resurrection, heaven, and hell and possibly purgatory are pillars of our beliefs. Honestly, I am not so sure of the afterlife or resurrection as described in Christian teachings. I do believe that I should lead a good moral life and if there is no afterlife, I will still thank our creator with my last breath for the wonderful opportunity in the life I was given. While still hoping to see you on the other side!

Chapter 42
Legacy

What is anyone's legacy? A legacy may be money or property given to another upon death in a will. It may refer to something handed down from an ancestor. So legacy can be an inheritance or part of your heritage. It can be something we inherit from past generations and pass to our future generations.

I hear ad nauseam about legacy in the final years of a US president's second term. You hear all about his legacy legislation or what does he want is legacy to be when he leaves office. I must tell you I could not care less. Most of our politician's real legacy is their narcissistic, egotistical, power-hungry personalities. Ralph Waldo Emerson wrote, 'The greatest gift is a portion of thyself.' I agree with Emerson that the most important gift we can give is of ourselves. That is a legacy worth caring about.

Have you ever thought about what kind of legacy you want to leave for future generations? Most often when people die there is a huge focus on the things they owned and who inherits their possessions. The idea of handing down ideas and values, small pieces of yourself, is a more important way to look at your legacy. What if you consider your legacy as to how you may have positively affected people's lives?

To help determine what you should focus on for your legacy first think about what legacy you received from your family? What principles or values did your parents practice and thereby leave behind for you? I know that my parents taught me there was dignity in hard work. They were very devout Catholics that made sure our religion was a part of our life and value system. I was taught the importance of education and the joy of reading. We had a close extended family with multiple generations full of hard-working religious individuals. Having parents that lived through the great depression and living the horror of World War II left us a legacy of strength, independence, and patriotism. They may have left little in possessions or wealth when they died but what a legacy of character!

I am sure that almost all people want to be remembered, loved, respected even revered. The idea of creating a legacy can be a powerful way to guide your activities during daily life. One legacy goal can be connecting your parents and grandparents' spirit and cultural values to your children and grandchildren's generations. The idea of strong roots and family values can give direction and stability for each coming generation.

On a more personal level, I have some strong feelings on what I hope I am accomplishing in my lifetime that will 'live on' after I am gone. I first feel that I must live a good virtuous and loving life to leave any worthwhile legacy for future generations. I realize I am not famous or someone that had any significant effect on the world. At best, I hope to leave a modest legacy that will be remembered by some people whose lives intersected with my life. I coached youth soccer for seventeen years affecting possibly over one hundred different players. I have always hoped that I taught them true sportsmanship and that they would think something like 'I want to find a good coach like I had for my children'. I hope I conducted myself in a way that improved their sports experience. My legacy is also my family: my wife, two daughters, and three grandchildren. I try to make myself fully available and active in my family's lives being the best that I can be as a husband, father, and grandfather. I also hope that I am leaving a legacy as a good employee, fellow worker, good fair boss, and a person you could depend upon.

I have some ideas on how you can build a strong and meaningful legacy. First, live and pursue your life with passion and joy which will spill over and raise the spirits of those around you. Share your time by coaching, mentoring, or volunteering. The more you give of yourself the more you receive in return. Share a smile, tell a joke, make someone laugh and you make a person's life better. Laughing even improves a person's health, so the more you can bring big smiles the more you add to others' lives. Work hard to support the activities of your friends and family when they are right for that person's life.

In some religions, the only real immortality is that which you give of yourself. Giving of yourself lives on in them and all successive generations until the end of time. If I have given even a little that has made an impact on my friends and family and will live on in them, that is all I can ask.

Chapter 43
Cancer

President Reagan famously liked to say that the nine most terrifying words in the English language are 'I'm from the government, and I'm here to help'.

I looked up the scariest words on the internet and got a bunch of nonsense such as nyctophobia: an abnormal fear of darkness. Other lists of scary words included virus, terrorist, abandonment, or trepidation. I disagree and if you stop and think about it, I should get little argument when I say that the scariest single word in the English language is cancer. Cancer is just plain scary. It is not the number one killer of Americans. Heart disease kills more people each year but does not strike fear as cancer does. Even with all our progress on many types of cancer, it remains among the scariest medical diagnoses a person can receive. I can tell you a cancer diagnosis is terrifying whether it is your first cancer or if you have had a previous cancer diagnosis.

The first time I had a doctor say I might have cancer and refer me to a specialist, I was virtually paralyzed with fear. It was early-stage skin cancer, very treatable, but still scary. The dermatologist I was referred to did not have an opening for over a month. That was even more upsetting, didn't they realize I had cancer? My wife, the nurse checked around, and we found someone that could take me the next week and they did a biopsy which confirmed cancer and quickly set an appointment to remove cancer which was in the center of my back. That was over fifteen years ago and since then I have had six more skin cancers removed and easily as many precancers frozen off.

When working with my dermatologist I asked the universal question why me? I was not a pool or beach guy, and I always wore a white tee shirt when out in the sun. I learned that a white cotton tee shirt only blocks 20% of the sun's dangerous rays. Today's fabrics are designed to block dangerous rays, wish someone had been making them sixty years ago. I go to the dermatologist every six months to make sure I catch anything new early. I will tell you any cancer diagnosis can overwhelm you. There are many types of cancer. Cancer can attack every part of the body, including the blood. It attacks every age from children to the elderly.

Numerous factors can influence your chance of getting cancer. These can include factors such as your genetics, cell mutations, hormones, and immune conditions. There are also external factors such as smoking, unhealthy diet, and infectious disease. We have made tremendous advances in the treatment of many cancers, and today there are several cancers if caught and treated early have a ninety five to ninety nine percent five-plus-year survival rate. The most curable cancers are cervical, breast, prostate, skin, thyroid, testicular, and Hodgkin's Lymphoma. If you do not catch the above early and allow it to spread these treatable cancers still rank near the top of the yearly deaths. There are some very deadly cancers with only limited treatment success including lung, colorectal, pancreatic, stomach, and brain. Any of these are more treatable if caught early. The good news is that the long list of cancer survivors continues to grow, as education, medical advancements, and early detection improve the success rates.

I was catching my skin cancers early and maybe getting a little complacent, but I was not ready when my PSA test during my annual physical came back high indicating prostate cancer, this was five years ago. My doctor put me on a heavy dose of an antibiotic because some elevated PSA tests are because of infections in the prostate, and it dropped back significantly but six months later it tested high again, so I was referred to a specialist. Since my prostate was not enlarged or showed no abnormalities, I was put on a six-month active surveillance program. Since prostate cancer is often a very slow-growing cancer you can often do this on early cancers. But every six months my PSA increased, and the doctor decided to do a new RNA test which is more accurate and precise than PSA tests. The test came back just above the level that indicated the presence of cancer. Next was a CAT scan that came back with no abnormality indicating little chance of cancer. However, my doctor did not feel satisfied with the conflicting data and suggested a biopsy.

Let me tell you a biopsy is no fun, they take twelve tissue samples from all areas of the prostate. The doctor said with the CAT scan and the small size of my prostate he felt there was less than a 30% chance they would find cancer. Well, they did find cancer cells in five of the samples, four with only 5% involvement and one with 40% involvement. That put me at a six on the Gleason scale, which is an early and possibly a less aggressive cancer. I had several options including staying on active surveillance since some prostate grows so slowly. I had time to decide what to do. To help with my decision, my doctor ordered a genome test which also confirmed a slow less aggressive cancer. At my next six-month checkup, my PSA had continued to go up, and we again discussed what I wanted to do. To be honest, I did not like the idea of another six months and another biopsy. Plus, it eats on you knowing that you have cancer growing in you however slow, so for me it was time to decide.

There are several treatments for prostate cancer including having it removed and radiation either internal with seeds or external radiation therapy. After several consultations, I picked external radiation therapy. My radiation doctor during a consultation said that with my age and cancer caught at this point and with radiation I had a 99.2% chance that something other than prostate cancer would kill me. To that, I responded that there was a 100% chance that something would kill me. Not sure he caught the humor. Anyway, I was already focused on living for as long as possible. I want to assure you I feel very lucky to catch cancer early and having very treatable cancers. I have lost family members and good friends to cancer, and I remember what they went through, so I in no way compare myself to others suffering from cancer.

I am a cancer survivor, but I do not feel worthy of that label. People of all ages with various stages of cancer are dealing with this disease and much tougher treatments such as chemo. They demonstrate courage and grace I can only imagine. I was fortunate that mine was caught early and is very treatable. I wish everyone could be so lucky. My life had been blessed and every day is even more opportunity for a new experience and a day to share with my family and friends. I am planning on living long enough to work on that bucket list and to hit that hole in one on some golf course I have yet to play.

Epilogue

Have you guessed why the title using 43 days? Well, if you have a relative or a close friend that has gone through low dose radiation treatment for prostate cancer, you would recognize the significance. The treatment program includes a surgical procedure placing location pins in the prostate followed a week later by a CAT scan for final measurements and then 43 radiation treatments.

The radiation treatments are organized for the same time each day Monday through Friday for 43 treatments. No treatments on holidays or if the machine is offline for maintenance or repairs. If you miss for any reason, it just pushes your final date out so when you start, do not plan on leaving on vacation the exact date you think you would finish.

Life goes so fast and if you want to make it seem to slow down, try planning on and going through this treatment program. I read somewhere a theoretical proof that life goes faster the older you are. The theory states that as you get older, each year is a smaller percentage of your life. When you are ten years old, a year is ten percent of your life. When you are fifty years old, a year is two percent of your life.

Another theory thinks that time passes faster when we are in a set routine like work, and when we are not learning anything new, or when we stay stuck in a pattern of boredom. So maybe the key to making time slow down is to have new experiences. Well, life slowed down for prostate cancer treatment, but I do not recommend we all try that as a way to slow down life.

Knowing that I would be pretty shut down for almost three months was the perfect situation to finally do some writing. My wife had pushed previously for us to each put some information down for our daughters about our lives and our family heritage. Since we both lost parents' young our daughters knew little about our roots and having moved a lot and had so many jobs that we felt we had a good story for them. It may have also been triggered a little when our oldest daughter applied for a government position, and we had to dig out information on all the legal residences as well as other information for the background security checks.

I have tried to write my rambling remembrances and ruminations every day during the treatments just for fun, and hopefully, my family might have a little fun reading this. I know that having a distraction like writing has made the treatment time go a little bit faster.

I do not apologize to the 'PC' police, the 'woken' or the 'cancel culture' crowd. I believe that a vast majority of us love this country and want to build it up not tear it down. Maybe a little bout with cancer would help some of the extremists put a little perspective into their life.

CPSIA information can be obtained
at www.ICGtesting.com
Printed in the USA
BVHW040915250122
627116BV00016B/471

9 781638 290643